THE GREEK TRAGEDY
IN NEW TRANSLATIONS

GENERAL EDITORS
William Arrowsmith and Herbert Golder

EURIPIDES: Orestes

D0011657

EURIPIDES

Orestes

Translated by
JOHN PECK
and
FRANK NISETICH

New York   Oxford
OXFORD UNIVERSITY PRESS
1995

Oxford University Press

Oxford   New York
Athens   Auckland   Bangkok   Bombay
Calcutta   Cape Town   Dar es Salaam   Delhi
Florence   Hong Kong   Istanbul   Karachi
Kuala Lumpur   Madras   Madrid   Melbourne
Mexico City   Nairobi   Paris   Singapore
Taipei   Tokyo   Toronto

and associated companies in
Berlin   Ibadan

Published by Oxford University Press, Inc.
198 Madison Avenue, New York, New York 10016

Oxford is a registered trademark of Oxford University Press

Library of Congress Cataloging-in-Publication Data
Euripides.
[Orestes. English]
Orestes/Euripides; translated by John Peck and Frank Nisetich.
p.   cm. — (Greek tragedy in new translations)
ISBN 0-19-509659-2
1. Orestes (Greek mythology)—Drama.
I. Series.
PA3975.07   1995   882'.01—dc20
94-39711

9 8 7 6 5 4 3 2 1

Printed in the United States of America
on acid-free paper

For Ingrid, Rebecca, and Alexander

EDITORS' FOREWORD

The Greek Tragedy in New Translations is based on the conviction that poets like Aeschylus, Sophocles, and Euripides can only be properly rendered by translators who are themselves poets. Scholars may, it is true, produce useful and perceptive versions. But our most urgent present need is for a *re-creation* of these plays—as though they had been written, freshly and greatly, by masters fully at home in the English of our own times. Unless the translator is a poet, his original is likely to reach us in crippled form: deprived of the power and pertinence it must have if it is to speak to us of what is permanent in the Greek. But poetry is not enough; the translator must obviously *know* what he is doing, or he is bound to do it badly. Clearly, few contemporary poets possess enough Greek to undertake the complex and formidable task of transplanting a Greek play without also "colonializing" it or stripping it of its deep cultural difference, its remoteness from us. And that means depriving the play of that crucial *otherness* of Greek experience—a quality no less valuable to us than its closeness. Collaboration between scholar and poet is therefore the essential operating principle of the series. In fortunate cases scholar and poet co-exist; elsewhere we have teamed able poets and scholars in an effort to supply, through affinity and intimate collaboration, the necessary combination of skills.

An effort has been made to provide the general reader or student with first-rate critical introductions, clear expositions of translators' principles, commentary on difficult passages, ample stage directions, and glossaries of mythical terms encountered in the plays. Our purpose throughout has been to make the reading of the plays as vivid as possible. But our poets have constantly tried to remember that they were translating *plays*—plays meant to be produced, in language that actors could speak, naturally and with dignity. The poetry aims at being *dramatic* poetry and realizing itself in words and actions that are both speakable and playable.

Finally, the reader should perhaps be aware that no pains have been spared in order that the "minor" plays should be translated as carefully and brilliantly as the acknowledged masterpieces. For the Greek Tragedy in New Translations aims to be, in the fullest sense, *new*. If we need vigorous new poetic versions, we also need to see the plays with fresh eyes, to reassess the plays *for ourselves,* in terms of our own needs. This means translations that liberate us from the canons of an earlier age because the translators have recognized, and discovered, in often neglected works, the perceptions and wisdom that make these works ours and necessary to us.

A NOTE ON THE SERIES FORMAT

If only for the illusion of coherence, a series of thirty-three Greek plays requires a consistent format. Different translators, each with his individual voice, cannot possibly develop the sense of a single coherent style for each of the three tragedians; nor even the illusion that, despite their differences, the tragedians share a common set of conventions and a generic, or period, style. But they can at least share a common approach to orthography and a common vocabulary of conventions.

1. Spelling of Greek Names

Adherence to the old convention whereby Greek names were first Latinized before being housed in English is gradually disappearing. We are now clearly moving away from Latinization and toward precise transliteration. The break with tradition may be regrettable, but there is much to be said for hearing and seeing Greek names as though they were both Greek and *new,* instead of Roman or neo-classical importations. We cannot of course see them as wholly new. For better or worse certain names and myths are too deeply rooted in our literature and thought to be dislodged. To speak of "Helene" and "Hekabe" would be no less pedantic and absurd than to write "Aischylos" or "Platon" or "Thoukydides." There are of course borderline cases. "Jocasta" (as opposed to "Iokaste") is not a major mythical figure in her own right; her familiarity in her Latin form is a function of the fame of Sophocles' play as the tragedy *par excellence.* And as tourists we go to Delphi, not Delphoi. The precisely transliterated form may be pedantically "right," but the pedantry goes against the grain of cultural habit and actual usage.

As a general rule, we have therefore adopted a "mixed" orthography according to the principles suggested above. When a name has been firmly housed in English (admittedly the question of domestication is often moot), the traditional spelling has been kept. Otherwise names have been translit-erated. Throughout the series the *-os* termination of masculine names has been adopted, and Greek diphthongs (as in Iphigen*eia*) have normally been retained. We cannot expect complete agreement from readers (or from translators, for that matter) about borderline cases. But we want at least to make the operative principle clear: to walk a narrow line between ortho-graphical extremes in the hope of keeping what should not, if possible, be lost; and refreshing, in however tenuous a way, the specific sound and name-boundedness of Greek experience.

2. *Stage directions*

The ancient manuscripts of the Greek plays do not supply stage directions (though the ancient commentators often provide information relevant to staging, delivery, "blocking," etc.). Hence stage directions must be inferred from words and situations and our knowledge of Greek theatrical conven-tions. At best this is a ticklish and uncertain procedure. But it is surely preferable that good stage directions should be provided by the translator than that the reader should be left to his own devices in visualizing action, gesture, and spectacle. Obviously the directions supplied should be both spare and defensible. Ancient tragedy was austere and "distanced" by means of masks, which means that the reader must not expect the detailed intimacy ("He shrugs and turns wearily away," "She speaks with deliberate slowness, as though to emphasize the point," etc.) which characterizes stage directions in modern naturalistic drama. Because Greek drama is highly rhetorical and stylized, the translator knows that his words must do the real work of inflection and nuance. Therefore every effort has been made to supply the visual and tonal sense required by a given scene and the reader's (or actor's) putative unfamiliarity with the ancient conven-tions.

3. *Numbering of lines*

For the convenience of the reader who may wish to check the English against the Greek text or vice versa, the lines have been numbered accord-ing to both the Greek text and the translation. The lines of the English translation have been numbered in multiples of ten, and these numbers have been set in the right-hand margin. The (inclusive) Greek numeration will be found bracketed at the top of the page. The reader will doubtless note that in many plays the English lines out-number the Greek, but he should not therefore conclude that the translator has been unduly prolix. In most cases the reason is simply that the translator has adopted the free-flowing norms of modern Anglo-American prosody, with its brief, breath-and emphasis-determined lines, and its habit of indicating cadence and caesuras by line length and setting rather than by conventional punctua-tion. Other translators have preferred four-beat or five-beat lines, and in these cases Greek and English numerations will tend to converge.

4. Notes and Glossary

In addition to the Introduction, each play has been supplemented by Notes (identified by the line numbers of the translation) and a Glossary. The Notes are meant to supply information which the translators deem important to the interpretation of a passage; they also afford the translator an opportunity to justify what he has done. The Glossary is intended to spare the reader the trouble of going elsewhere to look up mythical or geographical terms. The entries are not meant to be comprehensive; when a fuller explanation is needed, it will be found in the Notes.

Boston   WILLIAM ARROWSMITH AND HERBERT GOLDER

CONTENTS

ORESTES

INTRODUCTION

I

Orestes was the young man who killed his mother and got away with it. The matricide is first, the escape second, but the two belong together, particularly in Athens.

Even an Athenian who had never heard of the theater would still be likely to know that Orestes, on his way to salvation, made a stop at Athens. His arrival there had not only been dramatized on the Athenian stage, it had also been enshrined from time immemorial in Athenian religious ritual. During the second day of the festival of the Anthesteria, the Athenians drank their wine in silence, commemorating the time when Orestes, polluted by the blood of his mother, Clytemnestra, was received into their midst but given a separate table and not spoken to—all out of fear of the contagion he bore. On that second day of the festival, everyone in Athens acted as if they, too, were contagious, as if they were, in a word, Orestes themselves.

The young man who killed his mother and got away with it was also the son of Agamemnon, king of Argos, leader of the Greek host that conquered Troy. Agamemnon died the very day he returned in triumph from the Trojan War, stabbed to death in his homecoming bath by his own wife, who had taken up with her husband's cousin during his absence. Wife and lover then usurped the Argive throne, reducing the dead king's alienated daughter, Electra, to servitude and sending his son, the potential avenger, into exile.

Orestes, then, had reasons for killing his mother. She betrayed and murdered his father, married his father's cousin, deprived him of his home and his inheritance. Reasons enough, in a situation less charged. Primordial custom made the next of kin responsible for avenging bloodshed, but when the blood had been spilled by the survivor's own mother, what was to be done? The god Apollo, speaking from his oracle at Delphi, gave the answer: let the son kill the mother, come what may. The god would help him deal with the terrifying consequences.

But it was just those consequences that brought Orestes to Athens: he was a fugitive from the *Erinyes* (Furies), avenging spirits of his mother's blood. Apollo, who had commanded him to kill her, could drive the Furies from his shrine at Delphi, but he could not keep them off the track of their quarry. And so it was that the final settlement between Orestes and the Furies did not come about at Delphi under Apollo's auspices but at Athens under Athena's.

Deliverance at Athens, however, lay in the future. It is, for Orestes in this play (but not the audience in the theater), the hidden part of his own legend. Equally important is the part of the legend that is not hidden from him and the other characters: the history of this tormented family up to the moment the play begins.

II

The founder of the line, Tantalos, appears dimly to Electra in the prologue, more spectacularly in the great monody she delivers later, her own death song. The crime he committed remains undefined, but what it means to Electra is clear enough. It engendered further crime. The family curse begins with Tantalos.

His son Pelops resorts to treachery to secure his bride, then murders the man who had helped him win her. The victim, Myrtilos, who had wanted the bride himself, curses Pelops and his descendants.

As if on cue, the sons of Pelops, Atreus and Thyestes, fall into violence fueled by sexual rivalry. Thyestes seduces his brother's wife, Aerope, and with her complicity gets possession of the throne of Argos. Betrayed by his wife and cheated of his throne, Atreus returns to power with Zeus' help and then expresses the desire to make up with the brother who had wronged him. In the most notorious episode of the entire saga, he takes the two sons of Thyestes, butchers them, and feeds them to their unsuspecting father at a feast of pretended reconciliation. Thyestes, enlightened as to the nature of the food he has eaten, curses his brother.

The curse of Thyestes on Atreus takes hold in the next generation. Atreus' two sons, Agamemnon and Menelaos, both suffer as their father and uncle suffered before them: from infidelity, lust for power, and violence against their own flesh and blood. The stage is set when the two brothers marry the daughters of Tyndareos of Sparta, Clytemnestra going to Agamemnon, and Helen, famed for her beauty, to Menelaos.

Helen runs away with the Trojan prince Paris, precipitating the famous war. Agamemnon assembles the Greek fleet at Aulis and takes command of the expedition, his eyes on military glory and the fabulous wealth of Troy.

But one thing stands in his way: the goddess Artemis demands the sacrifice of his daughter Iphigeneia or the ships cannot sail. The ambition of the king stifles the affection of the father. Agamemnon cuts his daughter's throat over the altar so the winds will blow. Of all the reasons Clytemnestra has for hatred, this one alone comes close to justifying her murder of her husband. But the man who joins her in adultery and bloodshed has his reasons too. He is Agamemnon's cousin Aigisthos, son and avenger of Thyestes.

Stroke and counterstroke, crime leading to further crime, it all transpires in the context of political strife. These are the throes of a dynastic family caught in the struggles of greed, lust, and power, turning on itself and casting its subjects, the people of Argos and of Greece, into the toils of war.

Orestes, born into such a family, lives out its worst propensities. Violence against kin takes its most daring and pitiful expression when he kills his mother. But he does so at a god's behest and, according to tradition, the gods stand by him in the end. He is to be the last of the avengers. Or so the original audience, familiar with the traditional story, had a right to expect. As the play goes on, Orestes acts more and more, not less and less, like his predecessors. He turns, again, on his own flesh and blood. Greed, too, and the lust for power have not yet let go their hold on him. By play's end, he stands on the brink of destruction. Yet, from beginning to end, he has shown redeeming qualities, characteristics that might account for the interference of the gods in his behalf.

III

The usurpers of Agamemnon's throne had reigned for seven years when Orestes returned from exile and killed them. On that very day his uncle Menelaos came home at last from the Trojan War.

Such is the account we find in Homer. Euripides makes one alteration, crucial to his dramatic purposes: he has Menelaos appear on the scene not immediately but six days after Clytemnestra and Aigisthos have fallen in blood. A lot has happened in the meantime.

The Furies of Clytemnestra have launched their attack on Orestes, reducing him, by the time the play opens, to exhaustion. In addition, old enemies of his father have been at work inciting the people against him and Electra. A meeting of the assembly this very day will determine their fate. The most likely outcome is death by stoning. Menelaos has arrived in the nick of time.

"The treatment of the legend is without parallel," remarked an ancient critic.[1] The first new element we notice is the political danger threatening

1. Aristophanes of Byzantium *Hypothesis* (preface), 5.

Orestes. Much more than a novel touch, it enables Euripides to introduce two major developments, both of which take the play further and further from the story familiar to the audience.

First is the possibility, almost a certainty by the end of the play, that Orestes will not get out of Argos alive. When he returns from pleading his cause in the assembly, abandoned by Menelaos and sentenced to take his own life or have it taken from him, the play has come within an inch of the impossible. How will Orestes go to Athens, as everyone knew he did eventually, if, instead, he dies in Argos?

The second development is no less in conflict with tradition. Orestes' friend Pylades proposes getting even with Menelaos for his failure to help by killing his restored wife, Helen, the only person who means anything to him. Having arrived in Argos the night before, she is still within the palace, an easy target. There is only one problem, for the audience if not the characters: everyone knew that Helen lived happily ever after with Menelaos in Sparta. According to some accounts, she even became a goddess.

The suggestion to kill her is prompted by despair. Orestes would at least not die unavenged. But now Electra thinks of a plan that may enable them both to get even and to escape. In the prologue, Helen, afraid to venture out of doors, has sent her daughter, Hermione, to pay respects at the tomb of Clytemnestra. The girl is due back at any moment. Electra suggests taking her hostage, threatening to kill her if her father, Menelaos, does not move to save them. Helen's dead body, on display, would show they are in earnest.

By the final moments, Helen, contrary to everything known about her fate, will seem to have died and Orestes, contrary to everything known about his, will seem on the point of dying, taking Hermione, Electra, Pylades, and the palace itself down with him in flames.

IV

So much for the plot, a stunning combination of old and new. The characters, with the sole exception of Pylades, struck one ancient critic as "worthless."[2] Modern critics have expanded the negative judgment to include Pylades and have made it the basis of a nihilistic reading of the play. Produced in 408 B.C., two years before the poet's death, *Orestes* appears to be an indictment by Euripides of the age in which he lived. Although none of the characters makes what we would call a heroic impression, the ten-

---

2. *Hypothesis* 21–22. Although the comment is included in the *Hypothesis* attributed to Aristophanes of Byzantium (c. 257–180 B.C.), it may belong to Didymus (c. 80–10 B.C.): M. L. West, *Euripides Orestes* (Warminster, Wiltshire, Eng.: 1987), p. 178. (Hereafter cited as West.)

dency to view them as signs of Euripides' final despair of Athens goes too far.[3]

We hear from Electra first. Although it is Orestes who has borne the brunt of the Furies' attacks, Electra has been at his side all along. Her devotion to her brother is complete, perhaps the most appealing thing about her.

She also exhibits formidable presence of mind, an ability to meet the demands of the moment, however unpredictable. Although she keeps things moving in the present, she provides, along with the chorus, our only source of comment on the legendary past. Her comments have a distinctive flavor, however. She imagines Tantalos' punishment and the prodigies that occurred when Atreus and Thyestes struggled for power in terms suggestive of astronomical speculations and discoveries. We catch, in such moments, a hint of the new learning associated in Athenian public opinion with the sophists.[4]

Helen, the second character to appear on stage, emerges from the palace during the prologue, engages Electra in conversation, and goes back into the palace, not to be seen again until the climax. Although she never fades entirely from our minds, our interest in her intensifies once the conspiracy against her gets underway. Seldom has a dramatist accomplished so much with a character so little seen and heard.

Her daughter, Hermione, says nothing at her first entrance, when Helen summons her from the palace, and very little at her next appearance, when Electra coaxes her back in. We shall see her a third time at the climax of the play, standing on the roof with Orestes, who holds a sword to her throat. She provides the conspirators with the hostage they need to put pressure on Menelaos. That is her role in the plot. She fits, also, into the larger pattern of the legend, resembling the sons of Thyestes killed by their uncle and the daughter of Agamemnon sacrificed by her father—innocents who become the tools of vengeance or the pawns of power.

The chorus enters next. When it first approaches, Electra refers to it as the partner of her lamentations, suggesting that she and it belong if not to the same household at least to the same social class. We learn later that it consists of daughters of the noblest families in the city.

After Electra has delivered her monody, about two-thirds of the way through, it is up to the chorus alone to continue reminding us of the legendary framework in which the play is set. There would be nothing exceptional about that if the normal harmony between the legend and the

---

3. W. Arrowsmith, *The Complete Greek Tragedies IV* (Chicago: 1959), 191. (Hereafter cited as Arrowsmith.)

4. The Athenians, for example, mistaking Socrates for a sophist, also assumed he was interested in physics and astronomy.

unfolding action were maintained; but dramatic momentum now begins to sweep the characters toward a catastrophe radically different from anything the audience familiar with the legend of the House of Atreus would expect. The temptation to take these reminders (ll. 1611–13, 1620–21, 1627) as ironical asides by the poet, wry hints at the irrelevance of the myth to the dramatic action, ought to be resisted. The chorus has said nothing until now that even remotely suggests irony.

V

A good deal of what Euripides wanted Orestes to evoke is suggested by his most constant epithet: he is, from beginning to end, *tlêmon Orestes* (Orestes "the enduring," "the suffering"), the one who has dared (*etlê*) to do something terrible and must suffer terribly in turn. The word has active as well as passive connotations, and both are reflected in the overall structure of the play. In the beginning, Orestes is largely passive; in the middle, under the influence of others, he starts to become active; by play's end, he has taken the reins himself. The general movement resembles that of *Oedipus at Colonus* or *Samson Agonistes*.

This is not to suggest that Orestes makes anything like the heroic impression of a Samson or an Oedipus. He is, we need to remember, a young man on the threshold of adulthood. Like Hippolytos and Pentheus, two other Euripidean adolescents, he has unattractive as well as attractive features. Not all the qualities an ancient audience would have recognized in him enjoy the sanction of modern morality. In particular, his sense of honor and desire for revenge may make us uneasy. To help one's friends and hurt one's enemies: so runs the ancient Greek code of ethics. According to this code, Orestes, striking back at those who have wronged him, demonstrates his self-worth. It is a far cry from the Christian injunction to turn the other cheek, but it would have won the approval of the average Athenian. Nor would the original audience have been put off by the decision to take vengeance on Menelaos through his wife. On the contrary, the misogyny that fuels the attack on Helen, although it may not sit well with us, is yet another motivation that would have struck a responsive chord in the ancient Greek heart.

In Electra and the chorus, in Menelaos and Tyndareos, Orestes evokes anxiety and solicitude, circumspection and curiosity, horror and loathing. All these responses and the attitudes that attend them derive from the deed he has done and the price he must pay. The burden falls with crushing weight on the shoulders of so young a man, and as the play develops we watch him at first sink into despair and then try to save himself. The goodness or badness of his character may in the end be less relevant than the excitement he generates simply by being the person he is, faced with the situation Euripides has invented for him. What has been ignored in criticism seems to have made itself felt on stage. *Orestes* was Euripides' "most popular play, indeed the most popular of all tragedies."[5]

As for the unattractive aspects of his character, the personal traits that would have made the original audience uncomfortable about him, they are not the ones we meet in modern assessments of him. One critic says that he has "murder . . . in his heart,"[6] another calls him "a juvenile delinquent of a startlingly modern depravity."[7] This, again, goes too far. Orestes is a young man with a young man's failings, suddenly thrust into a world governed by passions he is ill equipped to deal with, passions that gradually infect him too, in complex ways, direct and indirect.

VI

The main lines of his characterization are brilliantly laid down in the scene in which he confronts his uncle Menelaos and his grandfather Tyndareos.

Menelaos enters first. Horrified, curious, he keeps his distance from his nephew, son of the man who has done so much for him. Before the conversation ends in a desperate appeal by Orestes for help, Menelaos has taken stock of the political situation in Argos. The people will not allow Orestes to inherit the throne of Agamemnon (ll. 441–42).

We do not know how Menelaos intends to respond to the appeal he has just heard, for no sooner has Orestes made it than Tyndareos enters. King of Sparta, father of Clytemnestra, and father-in-law of Menelaos, he has come to pay respects at his daughter's tomb. As next of kin to the murdered woman, he should be interested in securing her killer's punishment. Two factors, however, operate to keep him from active pursuit of vengeance.

In the first place, the murdered woman, like her sister Helen, was a notorious adulteress. Tyndareos is her father, but he has no cause to feel proud of the fact. In the second place, the man who killed her is no stranger to him. The intensity of his feelings (in stark contrast to the coolness so far exhibited by Menelaos) derives from disappointed love, felt on both sides (ll. 463–69). The emotional situation on stage could not be more explosive.

Surprisingly, it is Menelaos, not Orestes, who ignites the explosion. Tyndareos is disturbed to find Menelaos talking with his nephew. Only a Greek corrupted by foreign influences would have anything to do with a polluted person, an "outcast" (l. 484), Tyndareos calls him. In response, Menelaos attacks such inflexible adherence to custom and law, suggesting that Tyndareos, in his abhorrence of Orestes, shows unthinking conserva-

5. West, p. 28.
6. Arrowsmith, p. 188.
7. B. M. W. Knox, *The Cambridge History of Classical Literature I: Greek Literature,* ed. P. E. Easterling and B. M. W. Knox (Cambridge, 1985), p. 331.

tism and irascibility, two characteristics typical of old men. This stings Tyndareos, as well it might, and moves him to defend his position at length, arguing that his own attitude toward Orestes, contrary to what Menelaos says about it, is eminently sensible. After all, there can hardly be anything more senseless than matricide.

Orestes then comes forward to defend killing his mother, point by point, as an act that made sense. The emphasis, which may strike a modern audience as peculiar, derives directly from the posture adopted by Tyndareos, the prosecutor in the case before us. The drama of the moment is heightened also by the rhetorical challenge: it will not be easy to prove that killing his mother was, under the circumstances, a reasonable thing to do.

But in addition to appreciating the difficulty facing the youthful orator at this point, the original audience might well have felt a little uneasy about him. He has already, in his conversation with Menelaos earlier, shown a bent for sophisticated paradox and clever repartee. In coming forward now to defend the matricide itself, he resembles a figure all too familiar in Athens at the time, that of the young man corrupted by an education designed to give its pupils the power of making the weaker argument appear the stronger—just the sort of education Socrates would be accused of providing the aristocratic youth of Athens at his trial only nine years later.

The defense of matricide as a sensible act also holds particular dangers for Orestes. His troubled feelings about women have already surfaced well before Tyndareos arrives on stage: in the scene where he first wakes up and engages Electra in conversation. In that earlier episode, Electra tells Orestes that Menelaos has arrived and that Helen is in the palace. The mere thought of Helen touches a sarcastic chord in the brother, as it had earlier in the sister and does again now: the two of them wax eloquent on the theme of Tyndareos' daughters, "notorious throughout Greece" (l. 249). Electra, however, soon has reason to regret encouraging Orestes in this vein: he looks at *her* now, a woman too, capable, perhaps, of the same monstrous behavior. She notices the change coming over him, but it is too late: the Furies are attacking.

A similar pattern emerges in the clash between grandfather and grandson. First, the misogynistic theme: again and again Orestes brings up Clytemnestra's adultery with Aigisthos. It was that, more than anything else, that seems to have incited him to take action against her. Even the murder of Agamemnon gets less emphasis in his defense, tending to appear more as a natural consequence of female depravity (ll. 579–85) than as something with a possible motivation of its own.

So much for the theme. The effect it produces comes close to the one it had in the earlier scene, only now it is Tyndareos who attacks, not the

Furies. By the time he quits the stage, he has become the avenger he might not have been but for the provocation we have just witnessed, his grandson's insistence on rubbing in the one thing that bothers him most.

VII

Tyndareos leaves, determined to incite the Argive assembly to pass sentence of death on Orestes and Electra too. He adds a warning for Menelaos: should he intervene, he will pay a high price—he will no longer be welcome in Sparta. Wealth and power are now at stake.

The characterization of Menelaos was censured by Aristotle as more base than it needed to be for the purposes of the drama.[8] The fundamental dramatic desideratum here is the betrayal of the nephew by the uncle. That alone is required by the plot. Euripides could have motivated it simply out of Menelaos' fear to lose what he already has, his position at Sparta; instead, he goes a step further, adding what Menelaos stands to gain from letting his nephew down: the death of Orestes would secure the vacancy of the throne in Argos. Who but the late king's brother and now only surviving heir would sit upon it next?

But Menelaos' baseness gets another touch. He is, in addition to being a traitor and a coward under a woman's spell, a Spartan. The brief argument between him and his father-in-law pits one Spartan, old and conservative, against another, younger and full of innovative ideas. The contrast suggests that Spartans are not what they used to be. The old man in fact levels a charge at his son-in-law that would have suggested precisely that to the original audience.

Menelaos' contempt for ancestral ways results, Tyndareos says, from his travels abroad. He has picked up barbarian attitudes and been corrupted by them. The charge has a good deal of resonance. It chimes with the note sounded earlier, when Menelaos first appears on stage, arriving as conqueror of Asia (ll. 353–55). From that point onward, the Trojans of Homeric poetry continue to be confused with the barbarians of contemporary Persia, and Troy is the "Asia" conquered by Agamemnon and Menelaos. Before the play has ended, we shall see that Menelaos' household, Helen and her retinue now inside the palace, is infested with such Trojans turned barbarians.

At the time of production, and for some years before and after, one of the burning foreign policy issues under discussion at Athens was the role played by the gold of the Persian king in Greek affairs. It was Sparta that had been enjoying Persian support till then. Athens tried to replace her in the favor of

8. *Poetics* 1454a 28–29, repeated at 1461b 21.

various satraps, without success. Sparta continued to replenish her war coffers with barbarian gold. The satirization of Menelaos as an orientalizing fop must have gone over well with the Athenians. What were their Spartan enemies now but craven dependents of the Great King?

VIII

Orestes, knowing he has been betrayed, sinks into despair when Menelaos leaves. His spirits lift with the arrival of Pylades.

First and foremost a catalyst, Pylades has an immediate energizing effect on Orestes. He provides, also, a foil for Menelaos. The treachery of the uncle stands out in stark relief against the almost fanatical loyalty of the friend.

The contrast is a variation on a major theme of the play, with topical as well as purely dramatic interest. The original audience would surely have applauded Pylades' faithfulness, but not with the wholehearted fervor of the ancient critic who dismissed everyone else in the play as worthless. They would just as surely have noted a troubling similarity between this young man, so dedicated to proving, through bloodshed, his devotion to his comrade, and the young men, educated by sophists[9]—and bound together in loyalty by their membership in aristocratic clubs—who had played the role of assassins in the oligarchic seizure of the government in 411 B.C., only three years before the play was produced.

The Four Hundred had seized power by entering the Athenian council chamber with daggers hidden in their cloaks, accompanied by 120 young men similarly armed. Euripides may have had that scene from recent history at the back of his mind when he depicted Orestes and Pylades entering the palace, determined to obtain swords inside, hide them in their cloaks, and then terrorize Helen's retinue, killing any who opposed them (ll. 1175–78).

Earlier, on their way to the Argive assembly, Pylades tells Orestes he is not ashamed to appear in public not only walking side by side with the polluted outcast but holding him up, guiding his steps. He disdains what the mob may think of it (l. 840), as Menelaos, earlier, had looked down on Tyndareos' reservations about talking with Orestes. The reasons differ: Pylades acts out of loyalty, Menelaos out of what he would call intelligence, an enlightened attitude. But both express disregard of the common outlook. The antidemocratic sentiment occurs again later, when Pylades suggests killing Helen and Orestes bursts into praise. One

9. Pylades has not as much time as Orestes and Menelaos to display his sophistry. It does not matter: one near quotation of Gorgias on the primacy of seeming over being suffices, in combination with the other touches, to make the impression intended. See note to l. 820.

comrade like Pylades, he says, is worth more than the favor of the mob (ll. 1203–04).

IX

Comrades in aristocratic pride and disdain for the mob, Orestes and Pylades go off together, hoping to sway the popular assembly to their side. They are, like the assembly itself, a volatile mixture of the contemporary and the mythical. The combination of the two is one of the most fascinating features of Euripides' dramatic achievement in this play. But which comes first? Does the myth remind him of the climate of Athens at the time, or is it the other way around, the contemporary scene inviting a new presentation of the myth? Whatever the answer, contemporary history does not seem far removed from the ancient story as Euripides presents it.

Tyndareos' insistence on the primacy of law, for example, has a good deal of contemporary resonance. In 409 B.C. the Athenians began a revision of their laws. The year *Orestes* was produced, the law of Draco on homicide was being copied and put on public display. Political killings had paved the way for the revolution of 411 B.C. When the democracy returned to power, the body of one of the traitors, Phrynichos, was disinterred and cast out of Attica, and those who fled to the Spartans were declared outlaws. An imprecise but suggestive parallel between the citizens who struck at Athenian democracy and the young man who shed his mother's blood may well have figured in Euripides' thoughts as he composed the play. Tyndareos, at any rate, views Orestes as an abomination, an outcast.

The question as to what to do with those who have such crimes on their heads—when, if ever, to let them return to normal life—was anything but academic at the time. In July 410 B.C., just under two years before the first performance of *Orestes*, the Athenians passed a law making it legal to kill anyone who had been an enemy of the democracy, stipulating that to do so would not incur blood guilt. [10] The harassment of those who had participated in the coup of 411 B.C. continued for several years; it was still being lamented by Aristophanes as late as 405 B.C., in the parabasis of his *Frogs*. Three years before, in our play, Orestes and Pylades, "young aristocrats beleaguered and hounded to death by an enraged demos," [11] would have roused uneasy memories by their fanatical loyalty to each other; at the same time, their rescue by Apollo would have done more than merely fulfill the expectation that their persecution *had* to end short of their deaths. It would also have satisfied a feeling that it *should* end for the good of all.

10. The law of Demophantos, quoted in Andokides 1.96-97. Blood guilt is a major theme of the play.
11. West, p. 36.

X

Apollo's appearance at the end of the play, however, seems to have satisfied no one. It has been called "an apparent resolution which in fact resolves nothing"[12] even though, in fact, it resolves everything.

The gulf between what Euripides has done and what modern critics make of it results directly from the exaggeration of the baseness of Orestes' character. Once he has been cast in the role of a criminal psychopath, the god who rescues him loses all claim to respect. Apollo cannot be real. His appearance at the end must have left everyone in the theater depressed by the thought that reality is the chaos in Argos, and Argos equals Athens. It is mere myth or dream or illusion that descends from heaven in the guise of Apollo, bringing about a blatantly mechanical resolution of the all-too-human problems unleashed by the drama. And it is with those problems, not their solution, that the audience leaves the theater.

The play, on this view, has a modern, even absurdist, feeling about it. Euripides brings in a god to remind us that gods, if they exist, are *not* in the habit of rescuing people from the consequences of their own evil actions. The Athenians, of course, were perfectly aware of this. What reason could Euripides have for reminding them of it, if not to deprive the myth of its meaning and the god of his dignity?

It is easy enough to leave the play with such feelings of disillusionment. They accord nicely with our sense of Euripides' sophistication. Indeed, his popularity in modern times owes not a little to the invitation he seems to hold out to us: to read him as if he were a modern dramatist. To do so, however, requires forgetting a number of factors that would have conditioned the impact of the original performance.

In the first place, Apollo's intervention does not involve anything impossible or unprecedented. In the second place, it is absolutely necessary, both in itself and in its manner and timing.

Greek gods act in their own interest and at their own prompting. Orestes is unhappy that "Apollo takes his time" (l. 422), but he does not deny that it is his privilege to do so. More important, if Apollo did not take his time, we would have no play. His failure to fortify Orestes against his enemies in the beginning is the dramatic premise for everything that follows. By the same token, Euripides could not have composed the play if Apollo were not available to resolve everything in the finale. A play about to end with Helen apparently dead and Orestes going down in flames is inconceivable without a god to put a stop to it. Apollo (absent in the beginning and arriving at the end) is the cornerstone. Take him away and all collapses.

12. Arrowsmith, p. 190. Often repeated.

Orestes, however, makes one comment—his last utterance but one in the play—that might seem, at first, to confirm an absurdist interpretation. He admits to wondering at times whether the god prompting him to act was a god at all (ll. 1741–43). When, in the next breath, he says that all that is over now, and "everything has turned out well" (l. 1744), we may be tempted to take his new confidence for delusion. His old misgivings seem more like the sort of thing Euripides the ironist would want to leave us with.

But there are good reasons, remote and immediate, for hesitating to take Orestes' words ironically. To deal with the remote reasons first, even the feelings Orestes has expressed before in regard to Apollo are not as vehement as one would expect from the hero of a play in which the god comes in for a critical drubbing.

Orestes first mentions Apollo during the onset of the Furies' attack. It is an implicit cry for help (l. 259). Before the attack has ended, he orders the Furies to accuse Apollo's oracles (l. 277). He returns to the idea later, when the Furies have left. Apollo (through his oracles) told him to kill his mother and ought to bear responsibility for it (ll. 287–89).

The striking reflection that follows, that the dead Agamemnon would have pleaded with him not to kill his mother (ll. 290–95), is less an indictment of Apollo than a sign of Orestes' despondency. Apparently abandoned by the god who moved him to do what he has done, he wishes that he had not done it. The emphasis falls not on the act itself but on its futility (l. 294: it has not restored Agamemnon to life) and on its consequences (l. 295: his own desperate plight). We are dealing with two negative moments, but only one criticism.

There are no others from Orestes in the rest of the play, a fact that has not been appreciated. The example just described occurs, also, in private; Orestes confides his doubts to Electra, the person closest to him. Later, in conversation with the skeptical Menelaos, he defends taking the god at his word. He wants not to appear entirely naive for having done so, but the defense itself rests on traditional attitudes of mortal deference to the power of the gods who act, after all, if and when it pleases them (ll. 418–22). Finally, Orestes asserts the god's patronage as his most powerful defense in the debate with Tyndareos on stage (ll. 612–21) and, presumably, off stage as well in the assembly (ll. 992–93).[13]

The last mention of Apollo before the finale is made by the Messenger from the assembly. It is he, not Orestes, who concludes that the god has

13. See note to ll. 992–93.

abandoned him. When Apollo finally makes good on his promise to stand by Orestes, he has not come to the rescue of a youthful blasphemer.

So much for Orestes' feelings about Apollo up to the moment Apollo intervenes to save him. The immediate reason we should hesitate before attributing his misgivings and final confidence to irony or delusion is the way he expresses them. He says that at times he feared it might not be a god but a fiend, an *alastor*, prompting him to act (ll. 1741–43). The feeling is natural enough, given all the suffering and confusion that have come upon him since he obeyed Apollo's command to kill his mother. He might well have feared being overtaken by Clytemnestra's fate, both in the sense in which Tyndareos says he deserves it (ll. 505–8) and in the Aeschylean sense that he, too, may prove to have been only one more member of this family destined to embody an *alastor* or avenging spirit.[14]

The chorus at one point sees the whole line of Atreus under the influence of such a spirit (ll. 339–43); at another point, they see Orestes and Pylades as *alastores* about to destroy themselves and the palace of the Atreids (l. 1622). Orestes' recollection that he feared at times mistaking what was really an *alastor* for the god Apollo, far from implying an ironical presentation of the myth affirms its meaning one more time before the end. Orestes *would* have perished as his forebears did were it not for the favor of the gods. To the others they sent only *alastores;* to him they also sent Apollo, one of themselves.

XII

Whatever else we may think of it, Apollo's appearance at the end brings the play to the most spectactular climax in all Greek tragedy. Standing on a platform, the god addresses Orestes on the roof and Menelaos on stage. At ground level, in the orchestra, the chorus watches, silent till it speaks the closing formula. All four available regions of space are occupied: the ground, the stage, the roof, the sky.

The stage, moreover, is thronged with silent extras. Menelaos summons armed men to help him as he rushes the palace doors, sword in hand. The roof too is crowded: Electra stands to one side of Orestes, Pylades to the other, both holding torches. Orestes himself holds a sword to the throat of Hermione, who makes a fourth figure on the roof. A few moments after Apollo has stepped into view, bringing everything to a sudden halt, the radiant figure of Helen joins him on the platform.

"The play is one of those that enjoy popularity on stage," remarked the ancient critic,[15] and we can see why. Yet it was not only the extraordinary

---

14. Aeschylus *Agamemnon* 1497–1504.
15. *Hypothesis* 21.

tableau at the end that made it a hit with ancient audiences. Euripides' stagecraft and masterful employment of the conventions of the theater work to powerful effect from beginning to end. The play would have had a brilliance in performance that can only be suggested here.

It opens with the weary Electra keeping watch beside the bed on which her brother lies unconscious. The chorus enters, alarming her. Perhaps they will disturb Orestes and precipitate another fit of madness. The usual uneventful entry of the chorus thus becomes a miniature drama, intriguing in itself but also serving to prepare us for the attack by the Furies, which then ensues.

The attack itself involves more activity than an ancient audience was used to seeing occur on stage. Not only the symptoms of the madness (Orestes leaping about, hallucinating, aiming imaginary arrows at invisible assailants) but also the effect of its outbreak on Electra (who tries to restrain him, to get him to lie down on his bed again, only to be thrust aside, helpless before the onset of the attack) must have been spellbinding.

Perhaps the most striking combination of the familiar and the unexpected occurs later, when the conspirators have all entered the palace and the chorus is left in the orchestra, wondering what to think. There have been noises from within. Helen has cried out, apparently on the point of death. The audience knows that Helen cannot die, but the chorus does not share in this certainty. It waits for the doors to open, for Helen's body to be wheeled out or for someone to emerge from the palace and describe how she died. The Athenians would have witnessed such scenes in other plays many times before.

But instead the doors open and a Phrygian slave stumbles out, frantic, in fear for his life. It is from him that the chorus leader tries to elicit a description of what went on inside. The scene has its own dynamics, intriguing in themselves, but they are enhanced when we take the conventions of the tragic theater into account.

Here is a messenger, the second to appear in the play. The first comported himself in the conventional manner. He came with news and gave it without hesitation, in iambic trimeter, the normal meter of spoken verse. When he was done, Electra had a clear idea of what transpired in the Argive assembly to which Orestes and Pylades were going when we last saw them. In contrast, the Phrygian, running away, scared to death, has to be stopped in midcareer and made to tell his story, and when he is done it is still unclear what has happened to Helen. Most surprising of all is his delivery. He does not speak, he sings. He is the only singing messenger in Greek tragedy.

We can hardly imagine the impact of such a novelty on the original audience. Yet it is not there for mere effect; it serves Euripides' dramatic purposes. Lyric, the language of emotion, may be more vague and allusive than spoken verse. The Phrygian sings because he is a bundle of emotions *and* because Euripides wishes to keep us in the dark as to the fate of Helen. What better witness of events whose outcome must be blurry than a hysterical foreigner? In addition, the Phrygian, threatened by Orestes' sword, manages to survive. So will Hermione on the roof in a few moments; so will Orestes himself. The Phrygian scene prepares us for the ending, which cannot be disastrous for any of the characters the dramatist has brought to the brink of disaster.

The poet's handling of stage properties is equally impressive. On a monumental scale, the palace stands in the center of the stage, a reminder, always, that we are watching a play about the notorious House of Atreus. Orestes and Menelaos engage in an unnerving duel to see who will inherit it. In the final moments, it is even in danger of destruction. And all the while Helen is inside, target of conspiracy, focus of uncertainty: Will she emerge again, alive or dead?

On a much smaller scale, once Orestes has gone to the assembly, we hear and presumably see no more of his bed. His passive phase is over, his active phase is in full swing. The bed on which he has been lying since the play began disappears with his passivity.

The early scenes of the play, all performed with the bed in view, enact a kind of overture. The quiet enjoined by Electra on the entering chorus gives way to the outburst of activity as the Furies attack Orestes. When the attack has ended, Electra goes into the palace to rest. A long stretch of dramatic time now elapses, during which very little action occurs on stage. We see Orestes make his first appeal to Menelaos, fall silent when Tyndareos enters, deliver a speech in response to his grandfather's attack, appeal to Menelaos again and then collapse on his bed only to be roused by Pylades to take his fate into his own hands. What happens afterward leads to an explosion of stage activity that makes the Furies' attack earlier seem mild.

No wonder *Orestes* was performed more often than any tragedy in the ancient world. Given the chance, it should do well in modern theaters too.

Sudbury, Mass.   F. N.
Easter 1994

TRANSLATOR'S NOTE
Because the tonalities of this play span a nearly operatic range, my guide and chastener, himself a seasoned translator and poet, has often shared my role. Our rendering is a full collaboration.

                          J. P.

ORESTES

CHARACTERS

ELECTRA sister of Orestes

HELEN wife of Menelaos

HERMIONE daughter of Helen and Menelaos

CHORUS noble Argive women, sympathetic to Electra and Orestes

ORESTES son of Agamemnon

MENELAOS brother of Agamemnon, husband of Helen, uncle of Orestes and Electra

TYNDAREOS maternal grandfather of Orestes and Electra

PYLADES companion of Orestes, betrothed to Electra

MESSENGER old retainer of Agamemnon's

PHRYGIAN one of Helen's slaves

APOLLO god of prophecy and purification

Line numbers in the right-hand margin of the text refer to the English translation only, and the notes at p. 93 are keyed to these lines. The bracketed line numbers in the running head lines refer to the Greek text.

Before the palace of Agamemnon in Argos. Orestes lies unconscious on a small bed, his sister Electra seated at his feet, keeping anxious and wearied watch. Time: six days after the killing of Clytemnestra.

ELECTRA No terror one can name—
            no suffering of any kind, no not even
            affliction sent by a god, is so terrible
            that human nature couldn't take it on.
            Tantalos, whom everyone called
            the happiest of men, the son, they say,
            of Zeus himself (and I don't mean
            to ridicule his fate), now
            shoots through the sky, terrified
            by the huge rock looming over his head.   10
            This is the price he pays, and why?
            According to the story, when he sat
            with the gods at the same table, a mere man
            banqueting with them as an equal,
            sick with insolence, shamefully
            he let his tongue run away with him.
            He had a son, Pelops, who in turn had a son
            born for strife with his own brother.
            But why do I have to go through
            the unspeakable again? Atreus   20
            butchered Thyestes' children and served them to him.
            I'll leave aside what happened after that
            and come to the sons of Atreus
            by Kretan Aerope: Agamemnon
            the glorious (if glorious is what he was)
            and Menelaos. Now Menelaos married
            Helen, whom the gods hate,
            while Agamemnon, lord of men, won
            Clytemnestra for his bride, the talk of Greece.
            Three girls were born to him—   30
            Chrysothemis, Iphigeneia, and myself, Electra—
            and a son, Orestes,
            all from one abominable mother

21

who wound her husband in an endless robe
and killed him, for reasons that a young woman
shouldn't mention. I'll leave them vague, then—
people know and may judge for themselves.
As for Apollo's injustice, what point is there
in my bringing charges against it? Still,
he persuaded my brother   40
to kill the woman who bore him.
Not everyone approves, but all the same
he obeyed the god: he murdered her, and I
did what a woman could, I helped him kill her.
     Since then he has been sick.
Orestes lies here savagely ill,
collapsed in his bed, and Mother's blood
whips him from it into fits of madness—
I say "Mother's blood" because
I dare not name the dread goddesses   50
who frenzy him. It's been six days, now,
since Mother's bloodstained body was cleansed by fire,
six days since he has eaten or washed himself.
Whenever the pain eases a little
and lets him come to his senses, he sobs there
buried under his robes, or sometimes
races from bed like a colt
bucking free of its yoke.
     Here in Argos they have decreed
that no one can shelter us,   60
or warm us at their fires, or even
speak to us, the matricides.
And this is the day set aside by the assembly
to determine if they'll stone the two of us to death.
But we still have some chance of escape.
Menelaos has landed from Troy,
rowing into harbor at Nauplia,
home at last from the war and long wanderings.
And the cause of all the bloodshed, Helen,
he sent ahead to our palace, waiting till darkness   70
for fear those who lost their sons at Troy,
seeing her in broad daylight, would stone her.

She's in there now, bewailing
her sister's death and the ruin of the house.
Yet she has some consolation:
her daughter, Hermione, whom Menelaos
brought from Sparta and left in my mother's care,
gives her delight, helping her to forget.
  But I am keeping watch,
I look everywhere, hoping to catch sight   80
of Menelaos, for our shaken strength
won't carry us through unless somehow
he saves us. A house brought down lies helpless.

Enter HELEN *from the palace.*

HELEN Ah, Electra, daughter of Clytemnestra and Agamemnon!
Still unmarried, after all these years,
how are you, and how is your brother?
Speaking with you won't contaminate me,
for I ascribe the crime
to Apollo. Yet I mourn for Clytemnestra, my sister—
I never saw her again, once I had sailed off to Troy.   90
Fate and madness, sent by the gods, drove me there.
But now I feel her loss, and the sting of sorrow.

ELECTRA Do I have to spell out, Helen,
what you can see for yourself?
Here I am, sleepless, watching over a miserable corpse—
he might as well be dead, he's hardly breathing:
I wouldn't ridicule his sufferings.
But now you've come, you
in all your happiness and your husband in his
as if to gloat on our misery.   100

HELEN How long has he been lying here?

ELECTRA Ever since he shed his mother's blood.

HELEN Poor man! And his poor mother, the way she died!

23

ELECTRA That's the way it is—evil overwhelmed him.

HELEN Would you do me a favor, though, Electra?

ELECTRA I would, but it depends: I must tend to my brother.

HELEN Won't you, just for me, go to my sister's grave . . .

ELECTRA My mother's grave, you mean—what for?

HELEN . . . to carry my libations and this offering of my hair?

ELECTRA Shouldn't you pay respects, yourself, at the tomb of a
                                                loved one?   110

HELEN Well, I'm ashamed to show my face in this city.

ELECTRA It's about time. You ran off in disgrace before.

HELEN There's truth in what you say, but no consideration.

ELECTRA So you feel shame among the Mycenaeans. I wonder why?

HELEN I fear the fathers of the dead left at Troy.

ELECTRA As well you may: they curse your name here in Argos.

HELEN Free me from fear, then: please, go in my place.

ELECTRA I couldn't bear to look on my mother's grave.

HELEN Yes, but how disgraceful, for a servant to take these things!

ELECTRA Then why not send your daughter, Hermione?   120

HELEN An unmarried girl shouldn't venture into the streets.

ELECTRA But she should visit the grave of the woman who raised her.

HELEN That's true, my dear. What you say is convincing.
　　　　Hermione, Hermione—

　　　　　　　　Enter HERMIONE *from the palace.*

My darling child, take these libations and my hair,
go to Clytemnestra's grave, pour out
the honeyed milk and the wine, and standing over the mound
speak these words: "Your sister bestows these,
who dares not come herself, living in fear of the Argives."
And bid her not to look unkindly   130
on me, you, my husband,
and this sorry pair, destroyed by the god.
Assure my sisterly observance
in all things due to the dead.
There, off with you now, perform the rites, then hurry back.

　　　Exit HERMIONE *offstage; exit* HELEN *into the palace.*

ELECTRA (*to herself*)
　　　　Nature! How your evil shows
　　　　　　in human beings!

　　　　　　　　　　　　　　(*to the audience*)

Did you see her,
barely trimming her locks to save her looks!

　　　　　　　　　　　　　(*to herself again*)

She's the woman she always was.   140

　　　　　　　　　　(*looking back at the palace*)

　　May the gods pour their hatred on you
　　for destroying me, and him here, and all Hellas!

　　　The CHORUS *approaches.* ELECTRA *rises in alarm.*

25

Oh no, here come my friends,
the women who echo my laments—
they'll wake him, start him raving, and me weeping.
    Women, step lightly, keep silence,
I know you mean well, but waking him
will destroy me.

Full entry of CHORUS.

CHORUS AND
    ELECTRA (*together*)

STROPHE A

CHORUS Softly, step softly, make no sound.

ELECTRA Away, away from the bed!   150

CHORUS See, we obey!

ELECTRA And please, speak as gently
            as the slender pipe.

CHORUS There . . . we'll whisper, like wind
            among the reeds.

ELECTRA Good. But lower still.
            And now, come closer, quietly,
                and very quietly say
                what you have to say,
            for at last he's at peace, he sleeps.   160

ANTISTROPHE A

CHORUS How is he, Electra? What happened? What's wrong?

ELECTRA He still breathes, but in gasps.

CHORUS What's that? I'm afraid.

26

ELECTRA Hush! If you drive sleep from his eyes,
        the one sweet grace he needs, you'll kill him.

CHORUS He took on horrors from the gods
        and suffers horribly.

ELECTRA   Ah, the pain of it!
        And the crime—yes, it was crime
        Apollo himself screamed for
        from the tripod of Righteousness,   170
        passing sentence of murder on our mother
        in return for murder!

STROPHE B

CHORUS Look at the covers—he's moving!

ELECTRA Yes, your cries disturbed him—hush!

CHORUS We thought he was asleep.

ELECTRA Circle back there, get back,
        away from the palace,
        and be quiet!

CHORUS But now he's resting. He'll sleep.

ELECTRA   So I pray!

(in the shrill intonation of a dirge, but softly)

        Oh majesty, Queen Night,   180
    bearer of sleep to toiling men,
    come, come from your darkness,
    lift yourself from your deeps, great power,
    and stretch wing to Agamemnon's palace,
        for pain and ruin are here,
        breaking, crushing us . . .

ELECTRA *turns to the* CHORUS *now approaching again.*

Too loud! Won't you quietly
    back away from his bed, my friends, won't you let
    sleep do its gentle work?

ANTISTROPHE B

CHORUS But tell us, what is in store—where will these evils end? 190

ELECTRA In death. What else? He won't even eat.

CHORUS Clearly, then, he will die.

ELECTRA Die at Apollo's hands—he sacrificed us
    with that black oracle of bloodshed
    overtaking bloodshed, to kill
    our father's killer, our mother.

CHORUS Justly!

ELECTRA   And hideously!

    You killed and died for it, Mother
    who gave me life, you destroyed
    Father and these children   200
    of your blood, leaving us lost,
    among the dead—Orestes
    a corpse already, and me
with nothing to live for, weeping
    through the long nights,
    sorrowing through time.

CHORUSLEADER Electra, you're next to him, look at your brother.
    His stillness frightens me.
    He may have died without your knowing it.

ORESTES *wakes suddenly, uncovering himself.*

28

ORESTES Oh precious charm of sleep, the nurse of sickness,   210
how sweetly you came to me when I needed you!
   Great queen of forgetting, wise power
the afflicted wisely pray to . . .

He looks about him.

   But where have I been? How did I get here? Nothing
of that comes back to me, it's been swept away.

ELECTRA Orestes, how glad I was to see you resting!
Do you want to get up now, shall I help you?

ORESTES Yes, give me your hand, help me up, and wipe
the scum from my eyes and mouth.

ELECTRA Let me, then: it's not beneath me   220
to tend my brother this way, with my own hands.

ORESTES Come, hold me up, and brush away
this matted hair. I can hardly see!

ELECTRA What a tangle of curls: how filthy! You've become
a wild animal, going so long without washing!

ORESTES Let me lie down again. When these seizures pass,
my arms and legs go limp, I have no strength.

ELECTRA There, now, when you're sick a bed is like a friend:
a good thing to have, but painful to need.

ORESTES Wait, prop me up again. And turn me around.   230
Helpless! The sick are so hard to please.

ELECTRA Do you want to swing your feet over and try
walking at last? A change can always help.

ORESTES Sure, if only to make a show of health—
it's better to seem so, even if you're not.

29

ELECTRA Orestes, I have something to tell you. Listen to me,
        while the Furies leave you some peace of mind.

ORESTES I hope your news is good news.
        I've had my fill of the other kind.

ELECTRA Our uncle, Menelaos, is here.   240
        His ship is anchored at Nauplia.

ORESTES Do you mean our troubles are over? Light at last?
        Our uncle here, who owes our father so much?

ELECTRA He's here, and—take this as proof of what I say—
        he's brought Helen with him, from the walls of Troy.

ORESTES He'd be a man to envy if he'd survived alone!
        He brings disaster with him, bringing that wife.

ELECTRA A fine pair of daughters Tyndareos sired,
        reviled at home, notorious throughout Greece!

ORESTES You, now! See that you don't take after them!   250
        You say you won't, but in your mind . . .

                                    ORESTES *rises, staring.*

ELECTRA Orestes! Now your eyes are wild . . . here it is
        again, the madness, and a moment ago you were fine!

ORESTES Please, Mother, no! Don't sic them on me,
        those girls with eyes of blood, with snakes . . .

ELECTRA Easy, easy now. Back into bed. You can't really
        be seeing them, however real they seem to you.

ORESTES I *do* see them. There they are, there, leaping at me!
        They'll kill me, Apollo—those bitch-hound faces
        and gorgon eyes, those priestesses of the dead! The
                                              goddesses!   260

                    ELECTRA *tries to force him onto the bed.*

Let go! You're one of them, you're one of my Furies
grabbing me, wrestling me down to hell!

ELECTRA I won't let go of you! I'll lock
my arms around you until it's all over . . .

                                   ORESTES *breaks free.*

Ah, what help can I call on now?
The gods themselves are against us.

                              ELECTRA *veils her face.*

ORESTES Bring me the horn-tipped bow, Apollo's gift,
the weapon he told me would drive the goddesses away
if they tried to terrorize me with their ravings.

                        ORESTES *draws the invisible bow.*

You may be goddesses,   270
but if you don't get back, out of my sight,
one of you is going to bleed
at a man's hands. Hear me?

                                        He shoots.

There! Don't you see the feathers
flash from his distance-devouring bow?
Go on, graze heaven with those wings!
Blame Apollo's oracles!

                                    He stops himself.

What came over me? Why am I
gasping? What drove me from bed? For now
the storm has passed, the great waves gone, it's calm again. 280

31

He sees ELECTRA *sobbing under her robe.*

Electra, why are you crying? Don't shroud your face.
The shame is mine, that you must feel my pain, you,
a young woman, having to put up with my sickness.
Don't weep that way because of me
and what I did! Yes, you agreed to it
but the blood, Mother's blood, was spilled by me.
It's Apollo I blame—
he put me up to the abomination, with everything he said
he cheered me on, but he's done nothing!
I now believe that if I'd gone to Father   290
and asked him face to face whether
to kill her, he would have begged me,
pleaded with me not to put a mother
to the sword. Could it bring him back to life?
Or not plague me as it does now?
But come, Electra, uncover your face,
don't cry anymore, no matter how bad it is.
When you see me losing heart, nurse me
out of my terror, my madness, and comfort me;
and when I hear you crying, I'll be there.   300
So should those who love each other help each other.
Go on into the palace, now, and get some rest,
bathe, eat, give your tired eyes some sleep.
If you abandon me, or fall sick caring for me,
I'm lost, I have no help but you—everyone else,
as you see, has deserted me.

ELECTRA   No, I can't leave—my place is here with you,
whether I die or live: it comes to the same thing.
For if you were to die, what would I do? A woman
without brother or father or friend,   310
how could I survive alone?
But if you think it best, of course I shall go in.
Meanwhile, you must lie down again yourself.
And if the terror and confusion come back,
hold them off, don't leave your bed.
Even an imaginary illness, a sickness

living only in the mind, feeds on the mind's belief
and so winds a man deeper in its toils.

ELECTRA *exits into the palace.* ORESTES *lies down.*

CHORUS

STROPHE

Wind-running and
    down-swooping   320

        goddesses of the abyss, banded together
        in dark orgies of weeping and keening,
        Eumenides robed in blackness
        who drum across the stretched air
        calling down blood punishment
        and punishment for blood shed,

        we pray, we pray you, free
        the son of Agamemnon
        from his seizing
        onspinning madness!   330
                        Ah, the pain
        you wrestled and were crushed,
        obeying the word Apollo

screamed from the tripod, in hushed
    precincts where they say the earth

    chambers her center.

ANTISTROPHE

Great God! What torment, what
    suffering will it end in,

        this gruesome agony driving you on?
        Some avenger
        hounding the whole line   340
        pours stream on stream of misery

33

into your sobbings, maddening you
for your mother's blood!

We grieve for you, we mourn!
Great human happiness cannot last—
some god topples it,
shakes the little sail
and punches the boat over
into the pounding waves, the swells of pain.

Or could we honor some other house   350
more than this one, sprung from Tantalos

and grown in the beds of the gods?

CHORUSLEADER   And now, here comes the king, Lord Menelaos.

Enter MENELAOS *with retinue.*

Welcome, O King, who launched
the fleet of a thousand ships against Asia!
No need to pray for good luck
in your coming: it stands beside you.
You have achieved what you asked from the gods.

MENELAOS   House of my fathers! Looking on you at last
and back from Troy, I am a happy man. Yet   360
I must greet you sadly, for never have I seen
more evils besiege, close in on a house!
Coming toward Cape Malea, I learned of Agamemnon's fate.
Out of the waves rose Glaukos
son of Nereus, sailor's prophet, unlying god,
who proclaimed it, right before my eyes:
"Menelaos, your brother lies dead
in the last bath his wife will draw for him."
I broke down at this, my men too,
and wept. But when I came ashore at Nauplia   370
and sent my wife on ahead, expecting
before long to put my arms

34

around Orestes and his mother,
finding them both well,
I heard the news—an old salt told me—
of the abominable murder of Tyndareos' daughter.
All the same, young women, tell me where he is,
Agamemnon's son, the man
who nerved himself to this horror.
When I left these halls on my way to Troy,   380
he was still a babe in Clytemnestra's arms
and so I wouldn't know him if I saw him.

> ORESTES *rises from his bed and steps forward.*

ORESTES Here I am, Menelaos, the man you're asking for.
I'll gladly testify to my horrors, but first
I appeal to you—

> *He kneels and touches* MENELAOS' *knees.*

I lack the suppliant's branches, so let me
hang my prayers here, let me implore you,
save me from disaster! You've come just in time.

MENELAOS O gods, what am I looking at? Someone back from the dead?

ORESTES That's right: I've been in hell. I'm there still.   390

MENELAOS The filth in your hair! Like a wild animal's.

ORESTES I'm finished. Nothing's left but my name.

MENELAOS Your eyes are frightening, burnt out.

ORESTES It's not my looks that disfigure me, it's what I've done.

MENELAOS What a ghastly sight! Nothing prepared me for this.

ORESTES Still, it's me, killer of my mother, such as she was.

35

MENELAOS I've heard about it. The less said, the better.

ORESTES However I hold back, the god has more.

MENELAOS What is it? What sickness is destroying you?

ORESTES My own mind. It sees what I did.   400

MENELAOS What does that mean? Be sensible, don't speak in riddles.

ORESTES Pain is one way of putting it, yes, pain . . .

MENELAOS A grim goddess, that one. But cures can be found.

ORESTES . . . and madness, the workings of my mother's blood.

MENELAOS When did it start? What day was it?

ORESTES The day I raised her burial mound.

MENELAOS Did it come over you at home, or at the pyre?

ORESTES The pyre, at night. I was waiting to gather her bones.

MENELAOS Was anyone else there, watching beside you?

ORESTES Pylades, who helped me kill my mother.   410

MENELAOS What kind of visions bring on the madness?

ORESTES I seemed to see three women. Women like the night.

MENELAOS I know who they are, but I'd rather not name them.

ORESTES They do inspire silence, those three. Best refrain.

MENELAOS It's they who drive you mad, for murdering your mother.

ORESTES But I can escape them. I've got a way out . . .

MENELAOS I hope you don't mean death. There's no sense in that.

ORESTES . . . through Apollo. He ordered me to kill her.

MENELAOS Yes, with scant regard for seemliness and justice.

ORESTES We're only slaves to the gods—whatever the gods are.   420

MENELAOS And what of Apollo? No help from him yet?

ORESTES Apollo takes his time. That's the way a god works.

MENELAOS How many days since your poor mother died?

ORESTES Six. The embers are still warm.

MENELAOS How quickly the goddesses visit her blood on you!

ORESTES Yes, they hound me, snapping at me, bringing me down!

MENELAOS Terrible acts have terrible consequences.

ORESTES I might have known better. Instead, I was true to my own.

MENELAOS You avenged your father, but what have you got to show for it?

ORESTES Nothing, yet. Help to come I call no help at all.   430

MENELAOS How are things with the city after what you've done?

ORESTES They shun us. They won't speak to us.

MENELAOS You haven't cleansed your hands of bloodshed, according to
custom?

ORESTES No. Wherever I'd go, they'd shut the door in my face.

MENELAOS Who's behind this? Who's hounding you out?

ORESTES Oiax, shifting the hatred of Troy onto my father.

MENELAOS I see: he's avenging the death of his brother Palamedes.

ORESTES Which wasn't *my* doing. But there's still a third blow.

MENELAOS From what quarter? The party of Aigisthos?

ORESTES Yes, them too. And they've got the city's ear.   440

MENELAOS Will Argos let you keep Agamemnon's scepter?

ORESTES How, when they won't let us keep our lives?

MENELAOS What action are they taking? Be specific.

ORESTES A vote, today—against us.

MENELAOS And you haven't gotten out of the country yet?

ORESTES We're penned in on every side by swords.

MENELAOS Whose? Personal enemies, or Argive troops?

ORESTES The whole populace, out for my blood. There you have it.

MENELAOS Poor man, you're at the end of your rope.

ORESTES But you can get me out, you alone.   450
         Come, now: here you are, flushed with success—
share some of it with us, your own kin
struggling to survive: don't hug it
to yourself, don't refuse
your own part in these troubles, but pay
your debt to our father, as you should.
Friends who aren't there when it counts
aren't worth the name.

CHORUSLEADER Here comes Tyndareos of Sparta,
         striving on at the stiff pace of age,   460

38

all in black and his hair shorn
in mourning for his daughter.

ORESTES Menelaos, I'm lost! It's Tyndareos. He's here!
Shame at what I did drives me from his sight, his
above all others! He raised me when I was little,
showered me, "Agamemnon's boy," with affection,
cradled me in his arms, he and Leda both,
making as much of me as of their own sons.
Heart and soul! I've not returned their love.

Moving aside, ORESTES *covers his head.*

Where is the darkness, where is cloud thick enough   470
to hide me from that old man's eyes?

Enter TYNDAREOS *with attendants.*

TYNDAREOS Where is my daughter's husband,
where may I lay eyes on Menelaos?
While I was pouring libations over Clytemnestra's grave,
I heard that he had come home,
landing at Nauplia safely with his wife
after all these years. Show the way,
I want to take his hand in welcome,
face to face at last.

MENELAOS Greetings, Sire, who shared your wife with Zeus.   480

TYNDAREOS There you are, then! Greetings also to you, my son.

He catches sight of ORESTES.

What's this! That snake who killed his mother, right here,
his sick eyes gleaming—I can't stand the sight of him.
Menelaos, you aren't talking with this outcast, are you?

MENELAOS What if I am? He's the son of a man who was close to me.

TYNDAREOS Agamemnon's son, you say, when he's turned out like this?

MENELAOS Yes, his son, and if his luck is down he's still to be honored.

TYNDAREOS All those years among barbarians have made you one yourself.

MENELAOS It's always been Greek to honor your own kin.

TYNDAREOS Yes, and not go in for lawlessness.   490

MENELAOS Only slaves do nothing but obey--that's the enlightened view.

TYNDAREOS You can keep such notions to yourself, I'll have none of them.

MENELAOS No, because your temper and your age don't make for good
sense.

TYNDAREOS Sense! There's some dispute about that in *his* case.
     Look: If everyone knows right from wrong
   then who on earth has shown less sense than he?
   To begin with, justice meant nothing to him:
   he spurned the practice followed by Greeks everywhere.
   When Agamemnon was struck down by my daughter—
   and I shall never excuse that atrocity—   500
   Orestes should have punished her, yes, but
   in a way respect for the gods demands:
   by casting her out. Then he would have kept
   a name for sanity, holding to law
   and righteousness. But as it is,
   his mother's own fate has claimed him.
   Yes, he was right to believe her damnable, but when
   he killed her, he damned himself twice over.
     Menelaos, let me put it this way.
   Suppose this man should be murdered by his wife.   510
   Their son in turn would then kill his own mother,
   and then his son in the next generation
   once again pays murder off
   with murder. I ask you, where would it end?
   Our ancestors found the way that works.

40

They commanded everyone to avoid contact
with a murderer, not even to look at him,
but to secure the favor of heaven again
by banishing, not killing him in turn.
The other way, someone would always   520
be taking the pollution onto his own hands.
    As for me, I loathe sinful women,
first among them my daughter, who slew her husband.
And Helen, too, your wife, I shall never approve,
I would not even speak to her.
Nor can I say you did well
going to the plain of Troy to get her back.
But with everything I can, I am committed
to defending the law and stopping this blood lust
that always turns men into beasts,   530
destroying cities and polluting the earth.

                    He turns suddenly on ORESTES.

And *you*, what kind of heart was beating inside you,
if you had any, when your mother begged you
to let her live, baring her breast to you?
These old eyes of mine saw nothing of that horror,
but even as I think of it now the tears well up . . .
    One thing bears out what I say.
You are hated by the gods themselves, you are paying
the penalty for what you did to her,
straying among terrors and driven mad. Do I need   540
witnesses to tell me what I can see for myself?

                    (*turning to* MENELAOS *again*)

So I hope it's clear, Menelaos:
don't go against the gods
by acting on your impulse to protect this man.
My daughter is dead. And she deserved to die.
But it was beyond all bounds for her to die at *his* hands.
    I've been a happy man in everything
except my daughters: in them I was unlucky.

CHORUSLEADER A man whose children are a blessing is fortunate.
Not so the one on whom they bring ruin and shame.   550

ORESTES *comes forward.*

ORESTES Sir, I am afraid to answer you
in a situation that guarantees offense.
If your great age were not before me,
I might not choke back my words. As it is,
your gray hair makes me tremble.
     As I see it, the law brands me an outcast
for killing my mother, but also embraces me
with another designation: my father's avenger.
What was I to do? Let's weigh
the factors involved, two sets of them.   560
Father sired me, while your daughter bore me;
his was the seed and hers the empty field.
In coming to his defense, then, I decided
to give priority not to the one who simply
nurtured me, but rather the one who gave me life.
And now the second point: your daughter—
shame prevents me from calling her "mother"—
took herself a man. It was a private wedding,
but not a decent one.
In saying this about her   570
I blacken my own name, but say it I will.
Aigisthos was her closet husband. I killed him
and added my mother's death to crown that sacrifice,
bringing pollution and treatment as an outcast
upon myself, but avenging my father.
     As for the grounds on which you and others
threaten me with stoning, listen to this:
they make me Greece's benefactor.
If women can muster the audacity
to kill their own lords, fleeing   580
to their children, baring their breasts
to excite "pity," as you call it,
then husband murder will count

42

for nothing, they'll resort to it
on the slightest pretext.
By my "dreadful crimes," as you loudly proclaim them,
I've put a stop to that sort of precedent.
　　In hating my mother, and killing her, I did justice.
She betrayed her husband while he was away from home
leading the combined Greek armies as commander-in-
　　　　　　　　　　　　　　　　　　　　chief—　　590
betrayed him, defiled their bed! And then, seeing
where all this was leading her,
she didn't punish herself; instead,
to avoid paying for her crimes,
she punished *him*, she killed my father!
　　It was *you*, Sir, who destroyed me—yes, *you*,
by fathering that evil daughter. Only because of her
outrageousness did I lose my own father and become
what I am: a matricide.
You see? Telemachos hasn't killed *his* mother, but then　600
neither has Penelope run around adding
husband to husband. Odysseus' wife
behaves. Her marriage bed stays undefiled.
　　By the gods!—or maybe I shouldn't mention gods:
it's they who execute blood justice.
But if I had condoned my mother's actions
by holding my tongue, what would my father's ghost
have done to me? Hated and driven me mad
with his own Furies, no?
Or do you suppose that my mother　　　　　　　　610
has gods of her own when he, wronged far more, has none?
　　And what of Apollo, isn't *he* there,
enthroned at Delphi, center of the world, giving
sure oracles to us all? When I killed
my mother, I was obeying him.
Treat *him* as an outcast, all of you, kill *him!*
I'm not at fault, he is. What was I to do?
Will the god not stand by his word
and cleanse me of pollution? How on earth
could anyone escape if the same god　　　　　　620

who commanded me to kill won't save me from being killed?
  Don't say, then, that what I did was terrible,
but that for me it has turned out terribly unlucky.

CHORUSLEADER Women are always getting themselves involved
in the lives of men, and seldom for the better.

TYNDAREOS Outrageous, are you? Refuse to curb your tongue,
do you? Answer in just the way
to gall me, will you? Well, then: you'll fire me
all the more to bring about your death!
I'll consider it an extra piety, a nice   630
companion to the act of homage
at my daughter's grave for which I came here.
The Argives are meeting in emergency session.
I'll go before them—they're eager enough—
and sic them on you, the whole city,
till I hear you both condemned to death
by stoning—you, and your sister.
Yes, her too! If anything, she deserves it more.
It was she who unleashed you against your mother,
baited you with tales to swell your hatred,   640
harping on the scandal of Agamemnon's death
and that affair with Aigisthos—I hope
it reeks in Hades, it was a stench in our faces here—
all fuel to the fire she kindled, your sister,
until the whole house went up in flames.
  As for you, Menelaos,
I have this to say, and I mean it:
if you care at all about being in my good graces,
don't go against the gods for the likes of him.
Let the people stone him to death! Try to prevent it   650
and you will never set foot in Sparta again.
Mark my words, and don't embrace
a blasphemer, or you'll put a lot of distance
between yourself and your more decent friends.
Men, lead me away from here.

                              Exit TYNDAREOS, *left.*

ORESTES Yes, go! What I have to say to Menelaos
I can say as I please, with your old age out of the way.

He turns to MENELAOS, *who is
now walking back and forth.*

Menelaos, why are you pacing up and down,
lost in thought? Is something troubling you?

MENELAOS Quiet. Something *is* on my mind. I don't know   660
which way to turn in this situation.

ORESTES Don't decide too hastily. Hear me out
first, and then make up your mind.

MENELAOS All right, go ahead. Sometimes it's better
to listen, at other times to talk.

ORESTES With your permission, then, I'll speak at length:
a longer speech makes for greater clarity.
    Menelaos, I'm not asking you
for anything of yours. Return, instead,
the favor you owe my father. Save   670
what I value most, of all that's mine: my life.
    I have transgressed.
What my guilt requires is a corresponding
transgression from you.
When my father Agamemnon assembled the invasion fleet
and went to Troy, he too was in the wrong
but not on his own account.
It was the sin of Helen, your wife's crime,
that he was mending. Like the true brother he was,
Agamemnon stood by your side, shield to shield,   680
and fought to retrieve your wife. Pay back to me, then,
what you got there: stand and fight, our savior
not for ten long years but one short day!
    As for what Aulis took, also through my father—
the sacrifice of my sister—I ask no return for that, you
need not lift a hand, yourself, against Hermione.

My situation being what it is,
the advantage must remain yours
and I must make allowance.
Offer, instead, my life to my poor father.   690
Do it to repay him, for if I die
his house, the house of Agamemnon, will be orphaned.
    Hopeless, you may say.
Exactly. But it's during crises
that we help each other, not in good times.
Who needs family when the gods make things smooth?
When those powers prove willing, it is enough.
    Everyone knows you love your wife.
I don't mean to disarm you
with flattery, Menelaos,   700
by begging you in her name.
Yes, beg: it has come to that.
What choice have I left?
I'm pleading for the house itself, root and branch.

                           ORESTES *adopts a suppliant's posture.*

Oh you who have my father's blood in your veins,
Uncle, imagine that in the dead underearth
Agamemnon hears this now, a ghost
fluttering over you, and that he finds
his voice in mine!

                                    (*rising to his feet again*)

        These are my claims. You've heard my case.   710
I'm pleading for my life, as any man would.

CHORUSLEADER I too, though I am only a woman, beg you
            to help them in their need, for you have the power.

MENELAOS Orestes, I, as you know, hold you
        in high regard and I very much want
        to share in your ordeals. Honor requires one

to take up a kinsman's troubles and carry them
to the end, if the gods grant the power, and even
to die, provided one's enemies die also.
But I'd have to get that power from the gods,   720
for I've come with barely a few fighting men,
worn out, myself, by the endless stress of wandering
and not able to count on the friends I left behind.
Force of arms, then, is not the way to win
ancient Argos. But if we try, by means
of gentle persuasion—*there* we have a fighting chance.
How can one hope to attain mighty ends
with meager resources?
Even wanting to do so is silly.
When anger sweeps the people and is still   730
rising in them, resistance
is like fighting a raging fire.
Yet if, biding his time, a man will calmly
ride out their fury, watching for the right moment,
the tantrum may blow over; and then you can easily
get what you want from them, as much as you want.
There is pity in the people, and powerful emotion—
picked prizes for the man with a sense of timing.
That being the case, I'll go and try to persuade
Tyndareos and the assembly not to carry things   740
too far. It's the same way with a ship:
when you rein her in, straining the ropes,
she heels over; let go, and she lifts again.
The gods hate overdoing it, so do the people.
I must save you, not by
resisting those who are stronger, but by being
clever. Using force, as you would perhaps
have me do, isn't the way—my spear alone
won't put your troubles to flight.
Nor would I ever choose the delicate approach   750
without good reason. As things are, if we're sensible,
we'll admit that we're the slaves of chance.

Exit MENELAOS, *left.*

ORESTES O mighty campaigner, when the cause is a woman,
but useless when it's your own kin, there you go
turning and running—can't wait to be off? And do
Agamemnon's claims count for nothing?
You lost your friends, Father, when you lost your luck!
   I am betrayed, I have no hope
of finding safety from death in Argos:
that uncle there was my last refuge.   760

        ORESTES *sinks back down on his couch, exhausted,*
            then looks up, sensing the approach of someone.

But wait! Here comes Pylades, my best friend
back from Phokis, running at full stride.
How good to see him! A person you can count on
in times of trouble is better than the sight of calm
to desperate sailors.

                    Enter PYLADES *from the right, running.*

PYLADES I came as fast as I could, rushing through town
when I heard the news—all too true,
as I saw for myself—that the citizens were meeting
to kill you and your sister, this very day.
What is all this? How are things with you?   770
How are you doing, comrade, friend, cousin—
for you're all these to me.

ORESTES We're lost. That—in a word—sums up my ruin.

PYLADES Then take me down with you. Friends are friends through
                                                   thick and thin.

ORESTES Menelaos is a traitor to me and my sister . . .

PYLADES I wouldn't expect a whore's husband to be much of a man.

ORESTES   . . . and might as well not have come back at all.

48

PYLADES It's true, then—he has returned? To this very place?

ORESTES At long last. But he wasn't long in dropping his own.

PYLADES And what of Helen? Did he come back with her on board? 780

ORESTES The other way around—she brought him.

PYLADES Where is she now, that woman who nearly wiped out Greece?

ORESTES Inside my palace—if I can still call it mine.

PYLADES And what did you ask from your father's own brother?

ORESTES Not to stand by watching the people kill me and my sister.

PYLADES Well, by god, what did he say to that, I'd like to know?

ORESTES He advised "caution," like the typical bad friend.

PYLADES What excuse did he reach for? That tells it all.

ORESTES Onto the scene walked that old sire of such fine daughters.

PYLADES You mean Tyndareos, furious, no doubt, because of
                                        Clytemnestra.   790

ORESTES Right. Menelaos preferred his "good graces" to my dead father.

PYLADES And he refused, point blank, to share in your struggle?

ORESTES He's not much with a spear, except among the ladies.

PYLADES You *are* in trouble, then. But does death have to be the out-
                                        come?

ORESTES That's for the people to decide. We're charged with murder.

PYLADES What will their vote determine? Tell me. I'm full of dread.

ORESTES Life or death. A few words, but they mean a lot.

PYLADES Then take your sister and escape! Leave these halls behind!

ORESTES But haven't you seen them? Armed men on guard, every-
                                                            where.

PYLADES I did find street after street fenced with spears.   800

ORESTES We're like a towered city holding besiegers at bay.

PYLADES Put some questions to me, now. I too am ruined.

ORESTES And who has added this to all my troubles?

PYLADES Strophios in his fury has banished me, my own father.

ORESTES In a private matter, or a public one? What was the charge?

PYLADES That I took your mother's blood upon myself. He calls me
                                                        "outcast."

ORESTES Just like me! All my sufferings, it seems, are to be yours.

PYLADES I'm not nimble Menelaos. I'll face what I must.

ORESTES What if the Argives want to kill you as well?

PYLADES It's not their affair; only Phokis has jurisdiction.   810

ORESTES Well, then: it's time we considered . . .

PYLADES   . . . what needs to be done?

ORESTES Suppose I went to the assembly and said . . .

PYLADES   . . . that you were justified . . .

ORESTES . . . as my father's avenger?

50

PYLADES   They may not welcome you with open arms.

ORESTES Should I grovel here instead, and die without speaking up?

PYLADES   A coward's way.

ORESTES Well, then, what should I do?

PYLADES   If you don't go, can you escape death?

ORESTES No.

PYLADES   And if you do, have you any chance of being saved?

ORESTES Perhaps, with luck.

PYLADES   Then that seems the better choice.

ORESTES Shall I go, then?

PYLADES   Yes. Even if you die you'll die nobly.

ORESTES You're right. That way I avoid cowardice.

PYLADES   More so than otherwise.

ORESTES My cause is just, too.   820

PYLADES   Pray only that it seem so.

ORESTES And some may take pity on me . . .

PYLADES   . . . considering your high birth . . .

ORESTES . . . and feeling outrage at my father's death.

PYLADES   I see it all coming.

ORESTES I must go, if only to die like a man!

PYLADES   Yes! I'll second that.

ORESTES But then there's my sister. Shall we tell her?

PYLADES   *I* wouldn't.

ORESTES You're right. There'd be a scene.

PYLADES   A bad omen, for sure.

ORESTES It's better, obviously, to say nothing.

PYLADES   And the time saved will help.

ORESTES Only *them, them* in my way—

PYLADES   What is it, what do you mean?

ORESTES The goddesses. They might drive me mad.

PYLADES   But I'll be right beside you.

ORESTES It's difficult, touching a sick man.

PYLADES   Not for me, with you.

ORESTES But take care: my madness might infect you, too!   830

PYLADES   Never mind that.

ORESTES Then you won't hold back?

PYLADES   Hesitation and friendship don't mix.

ORESTES Very well, then. Steer me on my way.

PYLADES   Gladly, with a friend's care.

ORESTES *rises from the couch, assisted by* PYLADES.

ORESTES And take me to my father's grave.

PYLADES   But what for?

ORESTES To pray to him for deliverance.

PYLADES   Yes. That he'll listen to.

ORESTES As for Mother's grave, I wouldn't look on it.

PYLADES   No—she was your enemy.

But quickly—or the Argives
may condemn you first: here, take my arm,
let my strength support your weakness,
and come with me right through town—
I don't care about the mob,   840
I'm not ashamed to suffer with you.
How will I ever prove my friendship if I don't
prove it now, when you're facing the worst?

ORESTES That's what I meant—friends are better than family!
A man whose mind mirrors your own, though there's
no blood tie, is better than an army of relatives.

Exit ORESTES *and* PYLADES *to the right.*

CHORUS

STROPHE

The vast prosperity, the prowess
vaunting itself through Greece
and on to Troy by the banks of Simois
has ebbed again for Atreus' house,   850
drawn down
by the old violence

bursting out among the Tantalids
over the golden lamb,
gruesome banquetings
and dismemberings of princes,
grief after grief
traded in blood until
now it envelops the divided
heirs of Atreus!   860

ANTISTROPHE

To call the hideous slashing
of a mother's flesh "good,"
and the lifting of the sword black with her blood
into the sunlight "noble"—
is this not
perverted piety
in those who do evil and madness in those who conceive it?
For in her terror of death,
Tyndareos' daughter cried out,
"My son, the gods have no part   870
in your daring.
Don't, for your father's sake,
steep yourself in infamy
forever!"

EPODE

Can earth show any sickness, misery, grief
greater than this dipping
of a son's hands
into a mother's blood?
That is what he did, and now
the Furies hunt him, now   880
his eyes, red with death, flash
this way and that, demented,
the son of Agamemnon.
The pity of it
when, seeing

her breasts, seeing her bare them
through gold-brocaded robes,
he slaughtered his mother for
        his father
in fate's grimmest trade!   890

                  ELECTRA *enters from the palace.*

ELECTRA Women! Am I right? Orestes ran away
in a fit of madness, driven by the goddesses?

CHORUSLEADER No, that isn't it. He's gone before the Argive people.

ELECTRA Oh no! Why on earth? Who persuaded him to do that?

CHORUSLEADER Pylades.

                Enter a MESSENGER *from the right.*

It shouldn't be long, though, before
this messenger tells us what happened to your brother.

MESSENGER Noble Electra! Daughter of Agamemnon,
hear what I have to say, unlucky though it is.

ELECTRA We're lost, then! Your words are all too clear.

MESSENGER The Pelasgians have decreed that your brother,   900
and you with him, poor woman, must die today.

ELECTRA It has come, the thing I've dreaded so long,
wasting away in fears of the future. It has come!
    But enough of that. Tell me about the trial.
When the Argives condemned us, what speeches
set them on giving us death?
Speak, Sir: is it stones or the sword
that will drive the breath of life from my body
when I and my brother go down together?

MESSENGER I happened to be coming through the gates from the fields, 910
wanting to see how things stood with you and Orestes.
For I always loved your father, and your house always sup-
ported me.
Peasant though I am I treat my friends nobly.
There was a crowd, then, going up the hill and filling the
seats
where they say Danaos called the very first assembly,
when Aigyptos pressed his claims there. Seeing
all the citizens gathering, I asked one of them,
"What's happening in Argos? Has some threat of war
come from our enemies? Why all this disturbance?"
And he said, pointing: "Don't you see Orestes there,   920
coming this way, to run his deadly race?"
And then I saw a sight I didn't expect and wish
I'd never seen: Pylades and your brother on their way,
one limp and dejected, the other suffering with him
like a brother, helping and watching over him.
When there was a full crowd, a herald stood up and asked:
"Who wants to speak to the issue, whether or not
Orestes must be put to death
for killing his mother?" And thereupon
Talthybios rose, your father's henchman at Troy.   930
Always one to kowtow, he spoke both ways at once,
extolling your father but disparaging Orestes,
interweaving noble sentiments with vulgar ones,
to the effect that customs established by Orestes
would not bode well for parents. And he kept on
glancing and smiling at Aigisthos' men.
That's his type: heralds always go for the main chance.
Him too, sidling up to those in power.
After that Lord Diomedes addressed them.
He advised the city not to execute you and your brother, 940
but to do what religion demands, that is to banish you.
Shouts of approval greeted this, but others dissented.
And after that there rose the kind of man
who will say anything at all to get his way,
patriotic when it suits him, a hireling,
ready to stir up a row with his loose talk,

56

sure to entangle his audience in some crime.
He exhorted them to kill you and Orestes
by stoning; and it was Tyndareos
who coached your executioner.   950
    Then another—not much to look at
but every inch a man—stood up and spoke against him.
Seldom seen in town or marketplace, he works the land
for himself, the kind of man our country relies on,
shrewd, though, and willing to press his points home.
Corruption couldn't touch him, not the way he's lived.
He said that Orestes, son of Agamemnon, ought
to be decorated for having dared to avenge
his father, to kill a whore and godless woman
who would have kept us from arming ourselves and going 960
off to war, afraid the stay-at-homes
would debauch the women while the men were gone.
He seemed to carry his point, too, at least
with respectable people.
                        And then
not a soul spoke up in support.
Your brother came forward
[and said, "Citizens of Argos,
holders and protectors of the land
given to our fathers by Inachos,
in *your* defense, no less than my own father's,   970
I slew my mother. For if women get away
with killing men, if they are condoned, you are all
as good as dead, or you must become
slaves, women's slaves. You will be doing
the opposite of what you should do.
As of now, the woman who betrayed my father's bed
has died. But if you are bent on killing me,
the law becomes a mockery, and any man
is as good as dead. Mark my words:
they won't hold back from it."]   980
But he didn't sway the crowd, for all his eloquence.
That scoundrel won—he carried the majority,
exhorting them to put your brother and you to death.
All that poor Orestes could do, to persuade them

to mitigate the sentence of public stoning, was to promise
that today both of you would take your own lives.
Pylades helped him to leave, weeping as he did so,
and other friends have joined them, commiserating, crying,
all on their way here now, a bitter spectacle.

So now you must prepare. Get a sword or a rope,   990
to make your way from the light. Noble birth has not saved
you,

not even Pythian Apollo throned upon his tripod
has been your savior, but rather your destroyer.

Exit MESSENGER. ELECTRA *and the* CHORUS *join in
lamentation.*

STROPHE

ELECTRA   Pelasgia! I take up
                                 the wail, raking
                     my face bloody and beating,
                                 beating my head
                     to render my due
                                 to Persephone of earth's dark,
                                 Queen of the dead!   1000

CHORUS   Let this land walled in
                                 by giants, taking
                     the knife to its hair
                                 in lamentation for
                                 the losses of this house—
                     for such, such is the pity of it—mourn
                                 those who are going to die,
                                 once captains of Hellas!

ANTISTROPHE

ELECTRA   For it's gone, gone,
                                 the line of Pelops erased,   1010
                     a house once envied for its happiness:
                                 the jealousy
                                 of the gods destroyed it,

58

and the votes cast
murderously by the many.

CHORUS   Little race living for a day
                       clamorous with pain,
               see how fate presses
                   steadily against your hopes!
                   With length of years   1020
               a man runs through his share of sorrows—
                   to live is to have
                       no certainty.

ELECTRA *moves to the center and sings the epode alone.*

EPODE

ELECTRA   Let me fly to the rock
               hanging in the sky
                       on chains of gold,
               spinning there
                       in whirlwinds, crag
               blasted from Olympos,

               to howl my black dirge   1030
                       to the great forefather
               Tantalos, founder of the house, what
                   horrors it has seen!
                               —the four whipped
                   horses shearing the air

               as Pelops drove
                       over the sea, flinging
               the corpse of Myrtilos
                   into the waves at Geraistos,
               hurtling above the slam of the surf,
                   the foam of the beaches.   1040

               From that the curse came
                   into our house!

59

Spawned in the flocks of Hermes,
that fleece-gold lamb's back flared
its ruinous wonder through
the fields of Atreus, breeder of horses.

From that moment Strife
set the soaring
            chariot of the sun
on its lonely road to dawn
and evening both at once,   1050
            and sent the seven

Pleiades plunging
onto a different track, and then,
            dealing death for death,
            comes the flesh feast
named for Thyestes, and the bed
faithless Kretan Aerope
fouled with her couplings!
                                    until
            it all bears down
on me and my brother, driven   1060
            upon us by the fate
            in our blood.

CHORUSLEADER And now here comes your brother,
            under sentence of death,
            and Pylades, still faithful
            when others fall away,
            all that a brother could be,
            trace horse leading the sick man.

                        Enter ORESTES *and* PYLADES.

ELECTRA Brother! To see you on the verge of the grave,
            before the gates of the world below!   1070
            Looking on you for the very
            last time, I can't bear it!

ORESTES Quiet, Electra! Won't you accept necessity
without womanish wailing? It's painful, but all the same . . .

ELECTRA And how can I *not* cry? We'll never see
the sun again, not you and I, ever.

ORESTES Haven't the Argives done enough? Must you
be killing me too? No more talk about it!

ELECTRA Your youth, Orestes—your sorry fate, your
untimely death! You should *live*, and you can't.   1080

ORESTES For god's sake, don't make a coward of me!
I'll cry too, if I think of it too much.

ELECTRA We're going to die! It's impossible not to weep,
everyone counts his own death a sorrow.

ORESTES Today is the day. We must choose between
noosing a rope and sharpening a sword.

ELECTRA I want *you*, Brother, to kill me, don't let some
Argive do it, heaping insult on Agamemnon's house.

ORESTES It's enough having Mother's blood on my hands: I won't
have yours too. Choose your own way, and do it yourself. 1090

ELECTRA I choose the sword, then, and I won't lag behind you
in using it. But now, let me take you in my arms . . .

ELECTRA *embraces* ORESTES.

ORESTES Enjoy that empty pleasure, if in the face of death
people still enjoy embracing one another.

ELECTRA You are body and soul to me, Orestes,
all that's lovable, all that's sweet!

ORESTES Now see how you've melted me! Come,
let me hold you, why should I go on resisting?

Oh sisterly warmth, these embraces are the only
marriage bed and children we shall ever have!   1100

ELECTRA O that we could die by the same sword
and lie together in the same coffin!

ORESTES Nothing would please me more, but as you see
there's none of our family left, to bury us together.

ELECTRA Didn't he speak up for you, even to save your life,
Menelaos—that coward, who betrayed our father?

ORESTES Never showed his face. Pinning his hopes on the throne,
he took care not to save his brother's children.
        But come, let us die
in a manner worthy of the name   1110
and deeds of Agamemnon! I'll show the Argives
what nobility is, plunging a sword through my heart!
And you must dare the same.

                                    (*turning to* PYLADES)

Pylades, you be the one to judge
the way we die, and lay out our bodies;
bury us in one tomb, beside our father's.
And now, farewell. I go, now, to accomplish the deed.

                            ORESTES *moves toward the palace.*

PYLADES Wait! One thing, to begin with, bothers me
in what you've said: Did you think
I'd care to go on living after you die?   1120

ORESTES I assumed you would: Why must you die with me?

PYLADES You ask me that? What is life without your friendship?

ORESTES You didn't kill your mother, as I did mine.

PYLADES I helped you, though, and ought to suffer as you do.

ORESTES Go back to your father. Forget about dying with me.
      Look: you have a city to return to,
I have none. You have a home
to inherit, and the haven of great wealth.
There's marriage ahead for you, though not—
as I had pledged in honor of our friendship—   1130
with this ill-starred girl. Another woman
will be your wife and bear you children.

            ORESTES *makes as if to leave again.*

                    Farewell, then,
best of friends, while you can, and we cannot:
we dead are done with faring well.

PYLADES How far you are from knowing what I have in mind!
May the earth reject my blood, and the sky my soul,
if ever I betray you, and get off free myself!
Not only did I take part in the murder;
I was the one who planned everything
for which you're now paying the price.   1140
It's right for me to die with you
and with her: I said I'd marry her—
as far as I'm concerned, she's my wife already.
And how would I put a good face on things
if I went back to Delphi, the citadel of Phokis?
Tell them I was your friend before, but not
when troubles came? Impossible.
Our fates are intertwined, and since we must die,
let's see to it that Menelaos suffers with us.

ORESTES If only we could! I would die happy.   1150

PYLADES Then trust me, and don't use that sword just yet.

ORESTES All right, if somehow I can pay back my enemy!

PYLADES Keep your voice down. I put small trust in women.

ORESTES Don't worry: these women are here as our friends.

PYLADES Let's kill Helen—that will get Menelaos where it hurts.

ORESTES How? I'm ready, if we can bring it off.

PYLADES We'll cut her throat. Isn't she hiding here, in your house?

ORESTES She's in there, all right, putting Menelaos' seal on the
property.

PYLADES Not anymore, she isn't. Her new husband is Hades.

ORESTES And how are we going to kill her? She has her entourage. 1160

PYLADES What sort of entourage? I'm not afraid of any Phrygians.

ORESTES Ministers of mirrors and creams and perfumes.

PYLADES What? She brought her Trojan luxuries home with her?

ORESTES She always found Greece too small to suit her needs.

PYLADES No matter, slaves are nothing to a free man.

ORESTES Just let me do it. I'd gladly die twice.

PYLADES Same here, if I can see you avenged.

ORESTES Lay out everything in detail.

PYLADES We'll go in as if we're really going to kill ourselves.

ORESTES I follow you so far. But what comes next?   1170

PYLADES We'll weep and wail and tell her all our sorrows.

ORESTES So that she'll burst into tears, while gloating inside.

PYLADES Yes—and we'll be feeling the same way at the same time!

ORESTES What's the next phase of the action?

PYLADES We'll get swords and hide them here, inside our robes.

ORESTES But how do we dispose of her servants first?

PYLADES We'll scatter them, and lock them out.

ORESTES Right: and anyone who isn't quiet, we kill.

PYLADES After that, the deed itself shows the way.

ORESTES Killing Helen, you mean: I'm with you there.   1180

PYLADES Yes, you are. But listen, now, to the beauty of my plan.
         If we were putting a lady to the sword, one with a little
         character, her murder would be a disgrace. But
         as it is, she'll finally pay for emptying Greece
         of fathers and sons alike, and turning brides into widows.
         There will be a cry of thanksgiving, bonfires
         piled to the gods, blessings prayed
         on both of us because we shed that bitch's blood.
         No longer will they brand you "Mother Murderer." Instead,
         they'll crown you with the title, "Slayer of Helen who
                                    slew Hellas."   1190
         And Menelaos must not, no, must never thrive while
         your father and you and your sister die, and your mother—
         but enough said—he *mustn't* inherit your palace
         now that he's got his wife back through Agamemnon's spear.
         I'll be damned if I don't run that woman through!
         Even if we don't succeed in killing Helen, we can still
         set fire to the palace and die in the flames!
         One thing's for certain: dying nobly
         or nobly bringing it off, we'll win great fame.

CHORUSLEADER   The daughter of Tyndareos deserves the hatred   1200
               of every woman alive. She has shamed her sex.

ORESTES   Nothing's better than firm friendship, neither great wealth
          nor supreme power. And as for the mob, it's
          worthless in the tally next to one noble friend.
          You, no one else, laid the deadly trap for Aigisthos
          and shared every danger with me, and again it's you
          delivering my enemies to me, standing at my side!
          But I won't go on: praise too can be overdone.
          As I'm going to die, I want to do something
          to my enemies first—destroy my betrayers,   1210
          let them suffer pain who caused me pain!
          I am, after all, the son of Agamemnon,
          the man whose worth lifted him over all Greece,
          no tyrant, but all the same he had a godlike power.
          I shall not tarnish his name by dying
          like some slave, but yield up my life
          like a free man, and punish Menelaos.
          That alone would make us fortunate.
          And if we also escape, killing Helen
          and not dying ourselves, salvation   1220
          somehow falling our way—well, I pray for that.
          It's sweet, and costs nothing, to let desire find a voice.

ELECTRA   That's it, Orestes! and I can see it coming true:
          safety for you, and him, and me—all three.

ORESTES   Inspired words, but what do they mean?
          I've never known you not to have your wits about you.

ELECTRA   Then listen to me—and you too, Pylades.

ORESTES   Go on. Why hold back what's good to hear?

ELECTRA   Remember Helen's daughter?—as if I needed to ask.

ORESTES   Of course, Hermione. Mother took care of her.   1230

ELECTRA She's gone to Clytemnestra's tomb.

ORESTES For what purpose? And what's in it for us?

ELECTRA To pour libations over Mother's grave.

ORESTES And what's that got to do with our escape?

ELECTRA Take her hostage when she returns.

ORESTES How does that help the three of us?

ELECTRA Once Helen is dead, if Menelaos threatens you,
or him or me—we're in this together—
then say you'll kill Hermione. Draw your sword
and hold it against the girl's throat.   1240
If, seeing Helen's bloody body lying there,
he wants to save his daughter's life and gives his word
that he'll save *us*, then let the girl go,
let her run to her father's arms. But if his fury should
get the better of him and he tries to kill you, then
respond in kind, make as if to slit the girl's throat.
If he puts up a show of force at first, my guess is
he'll soften soon enough. He's neither brave nor strong.
There's my plan for saving us. I've said what I have to say.

ORESTES A man's intelligence, matched with womanly grace: 1250
how you deserve to live rather than to die!
Pylades, what a loss—or, if you both survive,
what a wife she'll make you!

PYLADES So be it! May she come to Phokis
honored by the singing on our wedding day!

ORESTES But when will Hermione return?
Everything you've said is fine, if only
we can trap that filthy father's cub.

ELECTRA I think she ought to be approaching
at any moment. She's been gone long enough now.   1260

ORESTES Good!

>Electra, you stay here in front of the palace,
>waiting for the girl to come. Be prepared,
>if anyone gets inside before the murder,
>to shout, or bang on the doors, or get word to us.
>Pylades, we'll go in and arm ourselves with swords
>for the final contest.

He makes formal supplication.

>Oh Father below, in the vast halls of night,
>your son Orestes implores you: come, come to our aid!

ELECTRA joins him:

ELECTRA Oh Father come, come if you hear underground
your children calling you, dying in your cause!   1270

PYLADES also.

PYLADES My father's kinsman, great Agamemnon,
hear my prayers also: save your own children!

ORESTES I slew Mother!

ELECTRA   And I took the sword in my hands!

PYLADES I set things in motion, I nerved them to act.

ORESTES I did it for you!

ELECTRA   And I did not betray you!

PYLADES Hear them reproaching you? Won't you save them?

ORESTES I've poured out my tears for you!

ELECTRA   And I my lamentations!

PYLADES Enough now! It's time for action.
         If prayers carry like thrown spears, piercing down through earth,
         he hears.

                              PYLADES *makes supplication.*

                   Oh Zeus, ancestral Father, and you, Awesome
                                        Justice, 1280

                grant success to Orestes, and his sister, and me!
                The three of us face one trial: we must live
                or die together in a single judgment!

                    Exit PYLADES *and* ORESTES *into the palace.*

ELECTRA *and*
     CHORUS *(together)*

                              STROPHE

ELECTRA   Women of Mycenae, friends,
                     first rank of Pelasgia's first city . . .

CHORUS   What is your wish, my lady?
                     In the city of Danaos, we stand by you still.

ELECTRA I want some of you posted on the road here,
             and the rest on the road there, to guard the palace.

CHORUS   Good lady, why?   1290
                     Why ask us to do this?

ELECTRA   I'm worried that someone, seeing
                     my brother poised for the kill,
                     will make our troubles greater than they are.

         Halves of the chorus follow their leaders to each side.

LEADER *of*
SEMICHORUS A *(speaking from the left side)*
                 Take up position, women! We'll watch this road
                 where day breaks . . .

LEADER of
SEMICHORUS B (*speaking from the right side*)
    And we'll guard this one, to the west.

ELECTRA   But look around! Keep scanning
                left and right,
           here and there and back again!

BOTH
SEMICHORUSES (*together*)
                           We're doing as you say. 1300

ANTISTROPHE

ELECTRA   Keep those eyes moving, now,
          and take in everything, everywhere!

SEMICHORUS A   Look: here comes someone! Who can he be,
          stalking about the palace—a hunter?

ELECTRA We're finished, then! He'll tell our enemies
        about our young lions, hidden, waiting to spring!

SEMICHORUS A   There's nothing to fear, good lady,
               the road is empty, after all.

ELECTRA (*to* SEMICHORUS B)
           How are things over there?
           Tell me whether   1310
           your side of the palace is still deserted.

SEMICHOURS B All clear. (*to* SEMICHORUS A) But keep a sharp lookout
    on *your* side too: ours is secure.

SEMICHORUS A It's the same here: no sign of trouble.

ELECTRA   I'd better go listen at the door.

                 ELECTRA *puts her ear to the door.*

BOTH
SEMICHORUSES (*together*)
            You in there! All's quiet!
            What's stopping you
                        from slashing the victim?

EPODE

ELECTRA They don't hear you! And I can't do a thing!
            Are they standing there
                        staring at her good looks,   1320
            their swords dangling?

BOTH
SEMICHORUSES (*together*)
            Any minute now, some Argive soldier
            will go for the palace to save her!

ELECTRA Keep your eyes peeled! This is no time to relax!

                        (*to each* SEMICHORUS, *separately*)

            You circle over here, you over there!

BOTH
SEMICHORUSES (*in process of changing positions*)
            We're on our way,
            we're looking all around.

            The SEMICHORUSES *merge and stop at the sound of*
                                    HELEN's *voice.*

HELEN (*inside*)
            Argos! Argos! Treachery! Murder!

ELECTRA   Hear that? Our men have their hands in it now!
            That shriek was Helen's!   1330

CHORUS   Zeus, Zeus, shoot your
            everlasting force into their arms!

HELEN Menelaos, I'm dying! Where *are* you?

CHORUS   Cut her down, kill her now—
            slashing with both your
                double-edged swords,
            strike, pay her back for leaving
                husband and father, slaughtering
            Greeks by the thousands, all those who fell
                cut down by the flash of steel   1340
            on the banks of Skamander,
                the river of tears!

CHORUSLEADER Quiet, quiet now! I heard a sound—
            someone on the road, approaching the house.

ELECTRA Just in time! Right at the middle
            of the killing, in she comes: Hermione!
                No more shouting now! Compose yourselves, seem to be
            at ease, and don't let blushing faces
            betray your knowledge of what's gone on in there.
            I'll look downcast myself, as if I didn't know what
                                    happened.   1350

Enter HERMIONE *from the left.*

ELECTRA My girl, are you coming back from laying wreaths
            at Clytemnestra's tomb, and pouring out the funeral wine?

HERMIONE Yes, I've secured the blessings of the dead.
            But when I was returning, still some distance away,
            I grew frightened. I heard an outcry from the palace.

ELECTRA What's happening now might well make us cry.

HERMIONE Say it isn't so! What is the news?

ELECTRA Argos has decreed that Orestes and I must die.

HERMIONE No, never! Not my own flesh and blood!

72

ELECTRA They have spoken. We stand under the yoke of necessity. 1360

HERMIONE Is that why there was crying inside, too?

ELECTRA Yes. He fell at Helen's knees, and cried aloud, begging . . .

HERMIONE Who fell at her knees? I can't follow you.

ELECTRA Poor Orestes, imploring her to save him from death, and me
                                                                too.

HERMIONE No wonder, then, the house broke into wailing.

ELECTRA Yes, what greater cause for outcry?
        But come, join in supplication
     with those near and dear to you!
     Go in, and kneel before your mother, Helen,
     fortune's darling, pleading with her that Menelaos   1370
     not let us die. My own mother raised you!
     Have pity on us, then, and lighten our burden.
     Enter the struggle with us—come, let me lead you in.
     You are the only one who can save us now.

                    ELECTRA *escorts* HERMIONE *to the door.*

HERMIONE Yes, yes, right away! You'll be saved
         if I can help it.

                 HERMIONE *enters,* ELECTRA *pauses in the doorway.*

ELECTRA   Comrades in there!
            Here is your prey: won't you seize her now?

                                            (*from within*)

HERMIONE Help! Help! What is this?

ELECTRA   Quiet!
            You're here to save *us,* not yourself.

(*to the conspirators*)

Grab her, grab her! Put your swords to her throat   1380
and keep them there. Let her father see,
now that he has real men to deal with instead of
Trojan cowards, what a coward has coming to him!

ELECTRA *goes in, shutting the doors.*
The chorus begins a chant.

STROPHE

Make a stir, sisters,
make a stir at the doors,
to keep the work of murder
from rousing the Argives, bringing them
in arms to the royal house,
before we can see for a fact
Helen's red corpse in the palace,   1390
or get the story from one of the servants!
The disaster's in motion: How will it end?
The gods in their justice have brought down
judgment on Helen
who filled Greece with tears
for the sake of deadly Paris, murderous
Paris of Ida, who drew all Greece to Troy.

CHORUSLEADER But quiet! Just now the bolts on the royal doors
were rattling. Yes, a Phrygian is coming out—
we'll learn from him how things are inside.   1400

Enter PHRYGIAN *slave, in panic.*

PHRYGIAN I have escaped a Greek sword,
running from death
in my barbarian slippers
past the cedar-timbered
Doric porticoes,
fleeing, as barbarians do,

out of the palace, out of reach—
O Earth, Mother Earth!
Ai! Ai!
How, O ladies of this land,
how to leave, winging my way   1410
to the glittering sky, or to the sea
spun in the arms
of bull-horned Ocean
as he circles the world?

CHORUSLEADER   What *is* it, servant of Helen, man of Ida?

PHRYGIAN   Ilion! Ilion!
the fruited, the sacred,
O Phrygian city and Mount Ida,
I raise this barbarian cry
in grief for you, struck down   1420
by one glance from that vision
of loveliness born of the swan,
the feathered glory, Leda's child
Helen, ruinous Helen,
avenging Fury perched
on the very battlements
built by Apollo.
Ai! Ai!
Lament, bewail
the shattered plain of Troy—   1430
O Ganymede, royal rider,
lover of Zeus!

CHORUSLEADER   Man, please, *one thing at a time:* What happened in
there?

PHRYGIAN   *Ailinon! Ailinon!* wail the barbarians,
striking up the Asiatic death chant, *Aiai!*
when the blood of kings
shed by iron blades of Hades
is spilled upon the earth.

There came into the palace—
   I shall now relate it, one thing at a time— 1440
    into the palace came
      two Greeks, twin lions:

   one called himself son of the late generalissimo,
    the other, Strophios' son,
    dangerous like Odysseus,
    brooding and treacherous,
    sure to support his friends,
    fierce when making his move,
      cunning in battle,
      and a murderous snake. 1450
Damn him for his
   cold-blooded schemes!

   Once they got inside, those two
   made their way to the throne
    of Paris' bride,
    and groveled there
    with tearful faces,
    clutching at her
    this way and that,
    wrapping their hands 1460
   around her knees, the two of them.

   Up, up leapt her Phrygian servants
   muttering one to the other,
    under the flail of terror

   that foul play was afoot—
    a few still uncertain,
    others suspecting
    that the serpent who murdered
    his own mother
    was, then and there, 1470
  leading the child of Tyndareos
    into the fatal
    nets of a trap!

CHORUSLEADER   And where were you? Already hiding somewhere?

PHRYGIAN   No, I happened to be standing
                     by Helen, wafting the ringlets on Helen's cheeks
                          in the Phrygian manner, with my
                     great round fan, softly fanning the air.
                          She was twirling the spindle,
                          letting the yarn fall to the floor,   1480
                               in her wish to sew together
                          the purple draperies
                          from her Phrygian spoils, to leave
                               as a gift at Clytemnestra's grave.

                     Orestes then addressed her:
                     "Daughter of Zeus, please, rise from your couch
                     and come across the room, to the throne
                          of Pelops our great forefather,
                          to our venerable hearth, where you'll
                          learn what I have in mind."   1490
                     He pressed and pressed her, and presently she
                          went along, unable to foresee
                               what lay ahead.

                     Meanwhile his accomplice,
                          that devil Phokian, was taking care
                          of the rest, snarling,
                     "What? Not out of here yet, you Phrygian scum?"

                     He locked some of us in this part of the palace,
                          others in that—some in the
                          stables, some in latrines,   1500
                     one here, one there throughout the house—
                          anywhere but near our mistress!

CHORUSLEADER   And then? What happened after that?

PHRYGIAN   Mother of Ida, mighty
                               mighty Mother,
                          what bloodshed I saw,

what crimes I witnessed
in those royal chambers!

On both sides, from the darkness
of their purple robes, they drew   1510
and held up swords, the two of them,
eyes shooting this way and that
to make sure no one was coming.

And then, like wild boars,
they squared off against
the woman, and began to close in.
        "Die," they cried, "You're going to die
and it's your coward husband
who kills you, he who betrayed
to death right here in Argos   1520
        his own brother's son!"
And she cried out, she shrieked,
her snowy arms beating her breasts,
her head ringing with blows—
and ran and ran, here and there,
        golden sandals flashing,

but Orestes, spearing his fingers through her hair,
        bracing his stance,
                his Greek boot firmly planted,
and twisting her head   1530
                onto her left shoulder,
was on the point of driving
deep into her gorge
                the dark sword.

CHORUSLEADER   And what were you Phrygians doing to help her?
                                                        Anything?

PHRYGIAN   Screaming and shouting, we smashed our way with crow-
                                                              bars
                through massy frames and doors

and out we came running
from here, from there,
one with stones, one with a bow,   1540
    one with sword drawn!
But against us came Pylades
invincible, like—like Phrygian Hektor, or Ajax,
wearing the famed helmet of triple steel:
I saw him once, saw him at the Skaian gates.
Then at swords' points we clashed!

And soon we showed overwhelmingly
how, in the heat of battle, Phrygians
are inferior to Greeks: one ran off,
one perished on the spot, another   1550
fled wounded, another
    fell to his knees begging for life.

We took cover in the shadows, or fell down dead,
    or sprawled on the floor, dying.

Then into the palace came
luckless Hermione, right at the moment
her poor mother was sinking
    to the floor to perish!

And like Bacchae in unholy rage, the pair of them
    ran up to her, a fawn of the forest,   1560
and got their hands on her.
Then spinning around they swung back
and went for Zeus' daughter—
                                but she was gone
and nowhere to be seen
    throughout the palace—
Oh Zeus and Earth, and Light, and Night!—
    stolen from their clutches
through the power of drugs, or ma-
gicians, or thieving gods,
    who can say?   1570

What happened after that
                    I don't know—I got myself
                    out of there
                              fast.
            And so, in the end, Menelaos
        who suffered so much, sweating hard at Troy
        to get his wife Helen back, suffered for nothing!

CHORUSLEADER   One thing on top of another! And there seems no end—
                                                                    look,
                    here comes Orestes running at full tilt, sword in hand!

Enter ORESTES *from the palace.*

ORESTES Where's the one who got away from my sword?

The PHRYGIAN *falls at* ORESTES' *feet.*

PHRYGIAN I bow before you, Lord, head to the ground like a
                                                    barbarian.   1580

ORESTES You're not at Troy anymore. This is Argos!

PHRYGIAN Wherever a wise man finds himself, living is sweeter than
                                                                    dying.

ORESTES You didn't, by any chance, shout for Menelaos, did you?

PHRYGIAN No, but to save *you,* a far greater man!

ORESTES Then even *you* think Helen perished justly?

PHRYGIAN Most justly, even if she had three throats to cut.

ORESTES You're flattering me, not saying what you feel.

PHRYGIAN Didn't she deserve it, for ruining Greece, Phrygians and all?

ORESTES Then swear you're not sweet-talking me: swear or die!

PHRYGIAN I swear by what I'd hate to lose: my very life!   1590

ORESTES *moves the sword closer to his face.*

ORESTES Were all the Phrygians as scared of steel as you are?

PHRYGIAN Take it away! Up close, it mirrors bloody murder!

ORESTES Afraid of turning to stone, as if you'd seen a Gorgon?

PHRYGIAN No, turning to a corpse. As for Gorgons, I don't know any.

ORESTES You're a slave. Why fear Hades, the great liberator?

PHRYGIAN Every man, even a slave, likes the look of daylight.

ORESTES Well said! Your wits have saved you. Back into the palace,
                                                        now.

PHRYGIAN You aren't going to kill me?

ORESTES   No.

PHRYGIAN   That's good to hear.

                              The PHRYGIAN *rises and makes
                              as if to go back into the palace.*

ORESTES Wait! I've changed my mind.

                              The PHRYGIAN *grovels again.*

PHRYGIAN   Sounds bad for me.

ORESTES Don't be a fool! I wouldn't stoop   1600
to bloody your neck! Why, you're neither a man
nor a woman! No, I came out here at first
to put a stop to your noise—
Argos is sharp-eared and quick to respond.
But now, let Menelaos return—I'm not scared
to get him back within sword range,

showing off those long blond curls of his!
For if he leads the Argives against the palace
to avenge Helen's murder, and doesn't save me, he'll see
not only his wife's dead body but his daughter's too!   1610

Exit PHRYGIAN, *left.*
Exit ORESTES *into the palace, bolting the doors.*

CHORUS

ANTISTROPHE (*delayed*)

Disaster, sisters! Another fight
brings this family down,
another Atreid struggle!
What should we do now? Try to warn the city?
Or keep silent? . . .
Silence is safer now.
Look, on the roof of the palace, clouds of smoke
shooting to high heaven, warning everyone!
They're kindling torches, to fire the great house
of Tantalos, pressing on, on in their struggle!
The end is always in a god's hands,   1620
turned as he pleases—
but how tremendous is the power driving these avengers!
The house has plummeted in bloodshed, plunging
to ruin with Myrtilos from his chariot!

CHORUSLEADER But here comes Menelaos, making for the palace in haste—
he must have found out how things are going now.
Atreids in there! Time to bar the doors!
A man riding high will trample anyone
who's already down, as you are now, Orestes!

Enter MENELAOS *with armed men.*

MENELAOS I heard what they did, and came—   1630
the terrors, the outrages! That pair of beasts—
inhuman, that's what they are. [The tale is that Helen
has not died, no, but vanished—an empty rumor

82

some fellow spluttered to me in his panic.
But that's only a fabrication by the matricide,
a preposterous story.]

>   Someone open the doors!

> (*A pause. The doors remain shut.*
> MENELAOS *turns to his attendants.*

All right, force them open! We must at least
save my daughter from those murderers
[and retrieve my poor, poor wife—
those who murdered Helen   1640
must die together with her, by my own hand!]

> ORESTES *appears on the roof with his*
> *sword at* HERMIONE's *throat, flanked by*
> PYLADES *and* ELECTRA *holding torches.*

ORESTES You down there! Hands off those doors!
Yes, I mean you, Menelaos, for all your rage. Keep it up
and I'll tear off one of these fine old blocks
and smash your head with it, spoiling the work
our stonecarvers lavished on these cornices.
Besides, the doors are bolted to keep you out.

MENELAOS What's this!? Blazing torches,
men posted on the roof, as if under siege—
and my daughter with a sword at her throat!   1650

ORESTES Want to go on asking questions, or hear from me?

MENELAOS Neither. But it seems I'll have to listen.

ORESTES I intend to kill your daughter, if you're interested.

[MENELAOS Murder piled on murder, now you've killed Helen?

ORESTES If only I had. The gods robbed me of the opportunity.

MENELAOS You kill her and then insult me by denying it?

ORESTES I hate to, but deny it I must. I only wish . . .

MENELAOS You only wish what? You're unnerving.

ORESTES That I'd pitched the filth of Hellas into Hades!]

MENELAOS Give me my wife's body, so I can bury her.   1660

ORESTES Ask the gods for that. I'll kill your daughter.

MENELAOS Will you? Pile corpse on corpse—the mother killer?

ORESTES The father avenger—whom you betrayed to death.

MENELAOS Wasn't your mother's blood enough for you?

ORESTES I'll never have enough of killing whores.

MENELAOS And you, Pylades, will you join him in this murder?

ORESTES His silence speaks for itself. I'll do the talking.

MENELAOS You'll regret it, too, unless you manage to fly out of here.

ORESTES We're not going anywhere. But we shall set the palace on fire.

MENELAOS What!? Destroy the house of your fathers?   1670

ORESTES Yes, so you won't get it. And then it's *her* turn, over the flames!

MENELAOS Go ahead and kill her, then! You'll have me to reckon with.

ORESTES If that's the way you want it . . .

                              ORESTES *lifts his sword.*

MENELAOS   No, no! Don't do it!

ORESTES All right, but quiet! You're getting what you deserve.

MENELAOS And you deserve to go on living?

ORESTES   Yes, *and* ruling.

MENELAOS Ruling! Where on earth?

ORESTES   Here, in the land of my fathers.

MENELAOS A fine sight, you at the lustral waters!

ORESTES   Sure—why not?

MENELAOS *You* making sacrifice before battle!

ORESTES   Are you fit for that yourself?

MENELAOS My hands are clean.

ORESTES   But not your conscience.

MENELAOS Who would ever speak to you?   1680

ORESTES   Whoever loves his father.

MENELAOS What about the one who loves his mother?

ORESTES   He's lucky.

MENELAOS That leaves you out.

ORESTES   Indeed it does: I have no taste for whores.

MENELAOS Take that sword away from my daughter!

ORESTES   Why? You're false to the core.

MENELAOS You really intend to kill her?

ORESTES   Now you're believable.

MENELAOS Wait! What do you want from me?

ORESTES   Go to the Argives, and persuade them.

MENELAOS Persuade them of what?

ORESTES   Not to kill us. Appeal to them.

MENELAOS Or you will kill my daughter?

ORESTES   That's the way it is.

MENELAOS Oh Helen, poor Helen . . .

ORESTES   Why not poor me?

MENELAOS I brought you back from Troy to have your throat cut!

ORESTES   If only it were so!

MENELAOS And I fought so hard.   1690

ORESTES   Yes. But not for my sake.

MENELAOS And now, this outrage . . .

ORESTES   For proving so useless when it counted.

MENELAOS You've pinned me.

ORESTES   You've pinned yourself, you swine.
                    But come, Electra! It's time to torch the palace!

And you, Pylades, most loyal of all my friends,
set fire to the roofbeams!

MENELAOS Land of Danaos, of the founders and their horses!
Come on, Argives, bring your weapons, hurry!
He's lording it over your whole city, forcing it
to let him live—him, with his mother's blood on his hands!

> MENELAOS' *men move toward the palace.*
> APOLLO *appears on a platform above the roof.*

APOLLO Stop, Menelaos! Sheathe your anger: 1700
it is I, Phoibos, son of Leto,
addressing you.
                        And you, Orestes,
with your sword poised over that girl,
stop, hear what I have to say.
        As for Helen,
on whom, mistakenly, you let loose your rage
at Menelaos, I have rescued her,
snatching her from your sword at Zeus' bidding.
For the daughter of imperishable Zeus must not perish—
she's to have her throne by Castor and Polydeukes   1710
in the heavens, and bring salvation to sailors.
        So much for Helen, then. Orestes,
you must leave the country, crossing to the plains
of Parrhasia, and there live out the cycle of one year.
The Azanians and the Arcadians
will name the place Oresteion in memory of your exile.
Proceeding then to Athens, stand trial against
the three Eumenides for your mother's murder. The gods,
presiding as your judges, will determine on the Areopagos
the strict and sacred verdict of your acquittal.   1720
Then, Orestes, it will be your lot to marry the woman
at whose throat you hold that sword: Hermione.
The man who thinks he'll marry her, Neoptolemos,
never shall, for when he ventures to Delphi seeking from me
requital for the death of his father Achilles,
a Delphian sword will kill him. And give your sister,

as you once promised, to Pylades. A happy life awaits him.
  Menelaos, let Orestes reign here in Argos
and go, yourself, to rule in Sparta,
enjoying the dowry of your wife, who has given you   1730
only endless trouble until now. Find yourself
another bride, and take her into your house
now that the gods, by means of this one's beauty,

                    (APOLLO *points to* HELEN, *now
                    joining him on the platform.*)

                                                have driven
Greeks and Trojans together in the press of war
to drain the earth of its human horde
proliferating in pride.
As for the Argives, I myself shall reconcile them
to Orestes: he is not to be held accountable
for murdering his mother. I made him kill her.

ORESTES Great Loxias! Those oracles of yours   1740
told the truth after all! And yet I kept on
shivering with fear, thinking what I heard
as your voice was really some fiend's. But no,
everything has turned out well, and I'm at your command.

                    He frees HERMIONE.

  Look here: I take my sword from Hermione, and
welcome marriage with her, when her father gives his blessing.

MENELAOS Helen, daughter of Zeus, farewell! I envy you
your happy home among the gods. Orestes, as Apollo
has commanded, so I obey: I give you my child in marriage.
Coming from a great house, and taking your wife
                                        from another,   1750
may you thrive in this alliance, and I with you.

APOLLO Let each of you now go to the place I have assigned,
and cease your quarrels.

MENELAOS   I can only comply.

ORESTES I feel the same. To this new dispensation, Menelaos,
and to your oracles, Loxias, I am reconciled.

APOLLO Go, now, each on his way,
honoring Peace, loveliest of the gods,
and I shall lead Helen to the halls of Zeus,
high among the fires of heaven.
There, by Hera and Hebe,   1760
the wife of Herakles,
she will be seated as goddess,
and men will forever pour
                their offerings
to her and the Tyndaridai,
        as she watches over
those who go down to the sea.

CHORUS   High and holy Victory!
                Shine on my life
                        and let me always wear the crown!   1770

NOTES ON THE TEXT
GLOSSARY

NOTES ON THE TEXT

This is a translation of the Oxford text of Gilbert Murray but it also reflects work done by recent textual critics—C. W. Willink and M. L. West in particular—my indebtedness to whom is profound and extensive: I could not record it in detail without changing the nature of these notes.

I have employed brackets at a number of points in the translation, not because I am certain that all the lines in question do not belong to Euripides but because that was the simplest way of enabling readers to envision the play with and without them. My reasons for suspecting them are briefly set forth in the notes, often with reference to fuller discussion by West and Willink.

5–16 Tantalos would have been familiar to the ancient audience as an abuser of the hospitality he shared with the gods. Homer (*Odyssey* 11.582–92) has him "tantalized" by food and drink forever out of reach, Pindar (*Olympian Ode* 1.56–60) has him writhing under a huge rock that ever threatens to fall on his head. In both cases he is in the underworld. Euripides chooses the rock but transfers it from the underworld to the heavens. This is a striking innovation, possibly suggesting a parallel between Tantalos, mythical sinner against the gods, and contemporary philosophers and sophists who attempted to account for reality in scientific or rational as opposed to religious or mythical terms. The "impiety" of such explanations was still keenly felt in the Athens of Euripides' day (see Aristophanes' *Clouds* and Plato's *Apology of Socrates*).

16 *he let his tongue run away with him* The exact nature of Tantalos' crime is left vague. Insofar as he incriminates himself not through action but through speech, he resembles a sophist. See previous note.

22 *what happened after that* Possibly an allusion to the incestuous union between Thyestes and his own daughter, Pelopia. Aigisthos, the son born of this union, conspired with Clytemnestra in the murder of Agamemnon.

93

34 *who wound her husband in an endless robe* Clytemnestra wrapped Agamemnon in a robe as he emerged from his homecoming bath, then stabbed him to death.

50 *the dread goddesses* The *Erinyes* (Furies).

59 *Here in Argos* Mycenae is the seat of Agamemnon's power in Homer, but it had been conquered by Argos in 467–66 B.C., and the tragedians tended to use the name Argos instead. Mycenae, however, belonging to epic tradition, still occurs (as at ll. 114 and 1284).

59 *they have decreed* The formulaic language would remind the Athenians of their own assembly. A body of citizens making sovereign decisions after hearing the arguments of various speakers is an anachronism in this play. Not so the issue they debate (see next note).

60–62 The ban against all contact with Orestes and Electra reflects their status as *polluted*. The problem how to treat polluted individuals is familiar in Homer and other literature (such as this play) set in the heroic age.

85 *still unmarried* An issue resolved at the end (ll. 1726–27).

85 *after all these years* Roughly eighteen.

267 *the horn-tipped bow, Apollo's gift* The bow seems to exist only in Orestes' mind; at any rate, we hear nothing further of it.

302 *Go on into the palace, now, and get some rest* There will soon be three speaking characters present on stage at once (Orestes, Menelaos, Tyndareos), one of whom must be played by the actor now playing Electra.

339–40 *Some avenger/hounding the whole line* The killing of Thyestes' children by Atreus (ll. 20–21) produced an avenging spirit (*alastor*) who, through the agency of Clytemnestra, struck down Atreus' son Agamemnon (Aeschylus *Agamemnon* 1501). Now a new *alastor* has arisen from Clytemnestra's blood to punish her killer, Orestes. All involved in the series of killings are either victims or embodiments of an *alastor,* or both. In this sense, "the whole line" descended from Atreus can be imagined, individually and collectively, as dogged by "some avenger."

355 *against Asia* The Athenians of Euripides' day were in the habit of conflating the Trojans of epic poetry with contemporary Asiatics, that is, barbarians (Persians, Phrygians, etc.).

364 *Glaukos*   Originally a fisherman who became immortal after he had eaten a magic herb. Euripides has made him the son of Nereus (the prophetic Old Man of the Sea) in order to reinforce his prophetic credentials.

386 *I lack the suppliant's branches*   An ancient Greek suppliant carried an olive branch draped in wool.

422 *Apollo takes his time. That's the way a god works*   The justice of the gods might take generations to reach fulfillment. So, for example, Croesus lost his throne because his ancestor Gyges had acquired it through murder five generations earlier (Herodotus 1.13).

436–40 Palamedes, Oiax's brother, was falsely accused of treason and put to death by the Greeks at Troy under Agamemnon. According to some sources, Oiax not only welcomed the murder of Agamemnon but also encouraged Clytemnestra to carry it out. Now that she and Aigisthos have fallen, Oiax and his allies hope to retain their influence in the city by getting rid of Orestes. The political situation briefly described by Electra (ll. 59–64; see note on l. 59) is becoming clearer. The ascription of antiwar sentiment to Palamedes in Vergil (*Aeneid* 2.84) may also be relevant: the people resent the loss of their loved ones at Troy in this play (ll. 115–16) as in Aeschylus' *Agamemnon* (ll. 445–51).

459 *Here comes Tyndareos of Sparta*   There will now be three speaking actors on stage, representing three generations of the family.

468 *their own sons*   Castor and Polydeukes. Only Castor fits the description exactly, Polydeukes being the son of Leda by Zeus.

480 *who shared your wife with Zeus*   See previous note.

483 *his sick eyes gleaming*   Tyndareos sees Orestes as *infectious*. Talking with him could be dangerous. Just such a primitive notion underlies the communal banning of murderers (ll. 59–62).

488 *All those years among barbarians have made you one yourself*   The Trojans of Homer are not "barbarians" in the later sense of non-Greek. Another instance of the anachronism common throughout this play (see note on l. 355).

   The institution of blood-guilt is one of the *nomoi* (customs, laws) recognized by Greeks everywhere. To disregard it is, in Tyndareos' view, to shed one's Greekness.

490 *Yes, and not go in for lawlessness* According to Tyndareos, Menelaos takes exception to *nomoi* (see previous note) that everyone else agrees are binding.

551 *Sir* Orestes addresses his grandfather as an old man (*geron*), respectfully here, disdainfully later (l. 596).

556 *outcast* (*anosios*), literally "unholy, unacceptable to the gods."

568 *took herself a man* In Greek a man *married* a woman, a woman *was married* to a man. Clytemnestra is thus imagined playing the man's part, Aigisthos the woman's, in a reversal of the normal roles.

582 *"pity," as you call it* Tyndareos had not in fact used this word in his indictment.

586 *my "dreadful crimes"* Again, the quoted phrase does not actually occur in Tyndareos' speech.

596 *It was you, Sir* The change in tone here marks a striking departure from defending himself to attacking his accuser (see note on l. 551).

600–603 Penelope's chastity is twice contrasted with Clytemnestra's infidelity in the *Odyssey* (11.405–61, 24.192–202). Word of it has evidently reached Argos, some three years before the return of Odysseus.

602 *husband to husband* The echo between Orestes' phrasing here and Tyndareos' at lines 513–14 ("pays murder off / with murder") is much more prominent in the Greek, where the syntax, meter, position and even syllabification of the two words involved in each case are repeated exactly, only the words themselves being different. One almost hears the taunt, *"Murder on murder* (*phonoi phonon*) is not the primary issue here: it only results from your daughter taking *husband on husband* (*posei posin*)."

604 *or maybe I shouldn't mention gods* The Furies come to mind.

619 *cleanse me of pollution* One of Apollo's major functions was to deal with pollution, both individual and collective.

634 *I'll go before them* Tyndareos, as a foreigner, has no right to address the Argive assembly. In the end, someone else presents his views (ll. 949–50).

650–51 Extremely important lines: Menelaos' self-interest is now in conflict with his duty to protect his nephew.

670 *the favor you owe my father* Agamemnon got Helen back for him.

684 *what Aulis took, also through my father* Agamemnon sacrificed his daughter Iphigeneia at Aulis. The circumlocution minimizes the horror of her death and Agamemnon's responsibility for it.

705–9 Highly emotional. Agamemnon's soul is in the underworld, yet it is also imagined as hovering in the air and even as delivering the words now uttered by his son.

732 *like fighting a raging fire* Here the people are a fire, at lines 733–35 a stormy sea, at lines 741–43 a ship. The confusion of imagery mirrors the discomfort Menelaos feels backing away from Orestes.

739 *I'll go and try to persuade* A promise not kept.

762 *running at full stride* Everything (including the meter: see next note) quickens with the arrival of Pylades.

766 The meter in the Greek text now changes from the stately iambic trimeter to the lively trochaic (literally, running) tetrameter.

771 *cousin* Pylades' father had married a sister of Agamemnon, making him and Orestes cousins.

781 *she brought him* Menelaos plays the woman's part here, like Aigisthos (see note on l. 568).

820 *Pray only that it seem so* This has a sophistic ring to it. Compare Gorgias DK82B.26: "Being is not apparent if it does not attain to seeming."

846 *no blood tie* Orestes has not forgotten that he and Pylades are cousins (l. 771). In comparison with their devotion to each other, all else is irrelevant. This is rhetoric, not lapse of memory.

854 *the golden lamb* When Atreus and Thyestes quarreled over the throne of Argos, a decision was to be made between them on the basis of who could produce a portent. Atreus hoped to win with a golden lamb that had appeared in his flocks, but Thyestes in the meantime had seduced and corrupted Atreus' wife, Aerope, who put the miraculous lamb from her husband's into her lover's possession. In this way Thyestes was proclaimed king. Zeus then intervened in Atreus' behalf, causing changes in the heavens that led to a new decision, Atreus becoming king and Thyestes going into exile.

855–56 *gruesome banquetings / and dismemberings of princes*   The later event is placed first: Thyestes fed on the flesh of his children who had been killed and dismembered by Atreus (ll. 20–21).

859–60 *the divided / heirs of Atreus*   Evidently, Menelaos and Orestes.

915–16 *Danaos . . . Aigyptos*   Sons of Belus, descended, in the fourth generation, from the union of Zeus with Io. Danaos fled from Libya to Argos (home of his ancestress Io) and Aigyptos pursued him there. In the trial alluded to, Aigyptos was either trying to force Danaos to marry his fifty daughters to his own fifty sons or the marriage had already occurred and Aigyptos was demanding justice for the murder of the bridegrooms by their brides on the wedding night.

927 *"Who wants to speak to the issue . . . ?"*   This would remind the Athenians of the formula used in their own assembly (see note on l. 59).

930 *Talthybios*   In the *Iliad,* one of Agamemnon's messengers.

939 *Lord Diomedes*   An important hero in the *Iliad,* where he is referred to as "Lord over Argos."

964–65 *And then / not a soul spoke up in support*   The silence of Menelaos at this point is deafening (see note on l. 739).

967–80   I agree with Willink (pp. 236–37) that the bracketed lines quoting what Orestes said in the assembly [Greek text 932–42] are likely to be the work of someone other than Euripides. We have already heard what Orestes has to say in his defense (ll. 551–623). What he is quoted as saying here is anticlimactic (picking up the misogynistic theme developed by the previous speaker, ll. 957–62), repetitious ("as good as dead . . . as good as dead" [l. 973 . . . l. 979]), and not particularly clear ("doing / the opposite" [ll. 974–75]). It may also be relevant that the entire speech can be deleted without disrupting the flow of thought ("Your brother came forward / But he didn't sway the crowd" [ll. 966 / 981]).

992–93   The messenger's parting words suggest that he heard Orestes plead Apollo's complicity before the assembly (as before Tyndareos at ll. 612–21); it is the argument's failure to move the people, not Apollo's failure to appear at Orestes' side, that is likely to be on his mind. This is the last reference to Apollo's complicity until the climax of the play.

993 *but rather your destroyer*   Plays (as often) on the similarity in Greek between the name Apollo and the verb *apollunai* ("to destroy").

1001–2 *this land walled in / by giants*   Literally Cyclopean land. The gigantic Cyclopes built the walls of Mycenae/Argos and Tiryns.

1024–25 *the rock / hanging in the sky*   For Tantalos and his punishment see note on lines 5–16.

1027 *spinning there*   Electra's language suggests familiarity with the Anaxagorean view of the heavenly bodies held in place by centrifugal forces.

1033–35 Poseidon had given Pelops a chariot drawn by winged horses.

1036 *over the sea*   Pelops is imagined driving from the island of Lesbos (home, in the version Euripides is apparently following, of Pelops' bride, Hippodameia) to Greece.

1037 *Myrtilos*   The charioteer of Oinomaos, father of Hippodameia. Oinomaos refused to allow his daughter to marry anyone but the man who could defeat him in a chariot race, the losers forfeiting their lives. When Pelops came to compete for Hippodameia's hand, Myrtilos agreed to help in return for enjoying first night with the bride. He then removed the linchpin from Oinomaos' chariot, replacing it with one of wax. Oinomaos perished in the race and Hippodameia married Pelops, who rewarded Myrtilos for his treachery by casting him into the sea.

1038 *Geraistos*   In southern Euboea, on the coast of the Myrtoan Sea, so named for Myrtilos who met his death there.

1041 *the curse*   Myrtilos, falling to his death, cursed Pelops and his descendants.

1043 *Hermes*   Father of Myrtilos, an appropriate avenger.

1044 *that fleece-gold lamb's back*   See note on line 854.

1049–50 *on its lonely road to dawn / and evening both at once*   A complex blend of mythological and scientific elements, typical of Electra's language here and elsewhere (see notes on ll. 5–16, 1027). "Dawn" and "evening" stand poetically for east and west. The opposite motions can occur simultaneously because they involve different perspectives: the sun travels east with respect to the stars in the zodiac (a recent discovery at the time of the play's production), west with respect to the earth. Presumably, it used to travel in the same direction as the other stars; now it is alone, not only in its journey across the daytime sky but also in its journey through the heavens ("its lonely road").

According to the traditional account, Zeus, taking Atreus' side in the dispute with Thyestes (see note on l. 854), caused the sun to set in the east. This was a portent superior to the golden lamb produced by Thyestes, and so it confirmed Atreus in his possession of the throne. Euripides has made the astronomical change associated with the crimes of Pelops' descendants permanent instead of temporary (the portent described above occurs but once). An original harmony, in which sun and heavenly bodies moved in concert, has been forever disrupted as a result of human wickedness.

1051–52 *the seven / Pleiades*   The constellation of the Pleiades does duty for all the stars.

1099–1100 The sentiment expressed is not perverse: Greek epitaphs for those who have died young often lament the failure to marry and have children.

1125 *Go back to your father*   Evidently Orestes views the alienation of Pylades and Strophios (ll. 804–6) as temporary.

1151 *that sword*   That is, the sword you were talking about (see l. 1112). It is clear from line 1175 that they have not yet procured the swords they will need.

1154 *these women are here as our friends*   The complicity of the chorus is required for dramatic plausibility. It is also conventional in Greek tragedy.

1160–65 These lines, together with lines 1176–78, prepare for the appearance of the Phrygian later (ll. 1399–1599).

1160 *entourage*   Barbarian attendants in the Greek (see notes on l. 355 and l. 488).

1161 *Phrygians*   Allies of the Trojans in Homer, often used of the Trojans themselves in later literature, as here.

1267–83 The act culminates in a brief evocation by all three characters of Agamemnon's ghost, surely intended to recall the elaborate scene in Aeschylus' *Libation Bearers* (ll. 306–509) in which Electra and Orestes and the chorus (Pylades is present but silent in that scene) form a similar trio calling on the ghost of Agamemnon for assistance in the killing of Clytemnestra. Here Helen is the intended victim.

1285 *first rank of Pelasgia's first city* The women of the chorus belong to the noblest families of Argos, just beneath Electra herself in social standing. This makes their complicity with the royal pair natural as well as conventional (see note on l. 1154).

1319–21 Electra's fear that Orestes and Pylades have been so stunned by the sight of Helen's beauty that they cannot carry out their intention of killing her recalls how Menelaos after the fall of Troy approached Helen with the intention of punishing her for her adultery, only to drop his sword at the sight of her breast. This, the most famous illustration of his uxoriousness, was depicted in art and mentioned in earlier and in contemporary poetry (*Little Iliad;* Ibycus; Euripides *Andromache,* ll. 627–31; Aristophanes *Lysistrata,* ll. 155–56).

1328 *Argos! Argos! Treachery! Murder!* The attempt on Helen's life occurs (in accordance with tragic convention) off stage during this scene, to be described on stage in the next scene.

1333 *Menelaos, I'm dying!* From here on to the moment Apollo appears with the deified Helen at the end of the play, every reference to what is occurring at this moment *could* be taken to mean that she has perished.

1341 *Skamander* The famous river at Troy.

1389–90 *before we can see . . . /Helen's red corpse* The display of the corpse will convince Menelaos that the conspirators mean business (see l. 1241).

1391 *or get the story from one of the servants* Anticipating what occurs in the next scene. Ordinarily the palace doors would open and the killers themselves emerge, showing their handiwork. Here the killing itself fits into a larger scheme: the corpse is meant for Menelaos' eyes, and he has yet to return. The chorus hopes either to dash in and catch a glimpse before he comes or to hear what has happened from a witness.

1393–94 *The gods in their justice have brought down / judgment on Helen* Serves to reinforce the impression that Helen has met her fate (an impossible outcome as far as the audience is concerned). The antistrophe answering this strophe does not occur until 1611.

1399 *a Phrygian* The Phrygian who now emerges from the palace is one of Helen's household slaves. As such, he would have reminded the Athenians of the

Phrygian slaves in their own households. He has, however, a number of more exotic features. He is not necessarily a eunuch, though Orestes' characterization of him as "neither a man / nor a woman" (ll. 1601–2) and his employment in the women's quarters suggests as much. At times in his aria and in the interchange between him and Orestes, he stands for the Trojans familiar in Homer (see note on l. 1161), at other times, especially when his effeminacy and cowardice come to the fore, he brings to mind Persians or Asiatics in general, the "barbarians" as the Athenians tended to see them. He is both the sort of enemy conquered by Menelaos and the sort of ally currently assisting the Spartans in their struggle with Athens (see my introduction, section VII). He is, finally, the only singing messenger in Greek tragedy. His song, as West (p. 277) describes it, is "articulate, high-flown, typical of late Euripidean lyric. Its incongruity in the mouth of such a character is part of the humour of this delectable scene."

1422 *loveliness born of the swan*   Zeus came to Leda (see notes on l. 468 and l. 480) in the form of a swan; Helen was born of their union.

1425 *avenging Fury*   For all his franticness, the Phrygian here sees things correctly: Helen *was* an instrument of the gods. See lines 91, 1733–36.

1426–27 *the very battlements / built by Apollo*   The walls of Troy.

1431 *Ganymede*   A Trojan prince, son of Tros. Zeus fell in love with him and took him off to Olympus.

1486 *"Daughter of Zeus . . ."*   See note on line 1422.

1578 *running at full tilt*   Orestes enters at a run, and the meter, appropriately, becomes trochaic when he speaks (see notes on ll. 762 and 766) and stays trochaic throughout his conversation with the Phrygian. The interchange between Orestes and the Phrygian is indeed lively: an ancient commentator condemned lines 1585 and 1594 as "too comic" and West (p. 283) remarked, "There is no funnier scene in Greek tragedy."

1585 *Then even you think Helen perished justly?*   Here and again at lines 1609–10 Orestes is clearly under the impression that he has killed Helen. West (p. 284), citing line 1689 as evidence that Orestes knows he has *not* killed her, remarked that we must either change the text of line 1585 or "convict Euripides of carelessness."

1585–86 The echo "justly? / Most justly" is reminiscent of similar interchanges between the braggart warriors and clever servants familiar on the comic stage. An ancient scholiast censured the interchange here as "unworthy of the tragedy and of Orestes' plight."

1594 The Scythian policeman in Aristophanes' *Women at the Thesmophoria* (1101–4) also does not know what a Gorgon is. Euripides adds a pun on the two meanings of Greek *kara* ("head" and "person"). An ancient critic called the line "too comic" (see previous note).

1609–10 *he'll see /. . . his wife's dead body* Orestes is evidently confident of being able to locate Helen though she was not there when he and Pylades went for her after seizing Hermione (ll. 1559–70).

1615 *Silence is safer now* The chorus is traditionally passive: it can only react to what the characters do.

1622 *these avengers* (alastores). See note on lines 339–40.

1623–24 *plunging / to ruin with Myrtilos from his chariot* The calamity threatening the house now is the direct consequence of what happened in the remote past: the descendants of Pelops were doomed from the moment Myrtilos uttered his curse (see notes on ll. 1037, 1038, and 1041).

1632–36 [*The tale is . . . a preposterous story*] The only identifiable source of Menelaos' information at this point is the Phrygian, whom Orestes let go just prior to boasting that he was not afraid of meeting Menelaos face to face (ll. 1605–6). It is unclear whether the gods (or some other mysterious agency) whisked Helen away alive or dead (ll. 1562–70). To represent Menelaos as convinced that Helen vanished *after* she was killed would spoil the calculated ambiguity of lines 1555–58. Apart from this, Willink (p. 340) points to a number of flaws in the portion of Menelaos' utterance bracketed here. The lines in question [Greek text 1556–60] may well have been interpolated.

1639–41 The preceding expression, "We must at least save my daughter" (ll. 1637–38), makes the addition of Helen (l. 1639) illogical (West, p. 288). This is another possible interpolation.

1654–59 Orestes himself is under the impression that Helen has perished (ll. 1585 and 1609–10). Why he should now disabuse Menelaos of the same impression is puzzling, for it is precisely what he would want Menelaos to think at this moment, even if he himself did not.
   Electra's plan envisions displaying Helen's body to convince Menelaos

that the conspirators are serious in their threat to murder Hermione if he does not cooperate (ll. 1237-49). Now that the body, or Helen herself, has disappeared, it would be just as easy for Orestes to claim that the gods robbed him of her corpse as it would be to claim that they rescued her alive, especially when Menelaos himself is certain she is dead.

Willink (pp. 342–43; on Greek text 1579–84) draws attention to a number of problems in phrasing. It is perhaps also relevant that the line in which Orestes first denies having killed Helen (l. 1655: "If only I had. The gods robbed me of the opportunity") opens with the same phrase as his reply to Menelaos' lament at line 1689 ("If only it were so"), a reply that could easily have given the cue to an interpolator here. (See note on l. 1689.)

1661 *Ask the gods for that* The words may be taken literally or figuratively: the gods know where Helen's body is because they have taken it away (the literal reading) or simply because they know everything (the figurative one). The figurative sense is the one intended by Orestes, but it is the literal that turns out to be the case (with the qualification that Apollo has taken Helen away alive, not dead).

1666 *And you, Pylades, will you join him in this murder?* The actor playing Pylades cannot answer this question. There are two speaking actors on stage now and a third (Apollo) about to arrive. The futility of the question is not apparent, however, until Orestes answers for Pylades. (See next note.)

1667 *His silence speaks for itself. I'll do the talking* The silencing of Pylades (loquacious until now) would have hinted at the arrival of another character (played by the third available speaking actor), possibly also at the impending resolution of the drama by divine intervention. Of equal importance, it draws attention to Orestes' independence: he is finally acting on his own initiative.

1683–84 These are extremely difficult lines to render without some awkwardness in English. In response to Menelaos' request to remove the sword, Orestes simply says literally "You are false." In response to the question Menelaos asks next, whether he intends to kill Hermione, Orestes answers, echoing his previous utterance, "There you are not false" (i.e., you hit the truth that time). The train of thought is as follows: Orestes would consent to remove the sword if he believed Menelaos capable of keeping his word, but he cannot believe him because he is, in his very nature (the Greek verb here emphasizes this), "false." When Menelaos then asks if he really intends to kill Hermione, Orestes cannot resist using the word "false" again, this time ironically. We have brought out what is implicit by adding the interrogative "Why" (i.e., Why should I let her go, since I cannot believe any promises you might make in return for her release?).

1689 *If only it were so!* To be taken as a reply to Menelaos' lament *in its entirety* (that he has brought Helen back only to see her slaughtered). It has been interpreted, however, as if it referred to the slaughter alone. West (p. 284) and, possibly, the ancient interpolator (see note on ll. 1654–59), understood it in this way. The slaughter of Helen, however, *and* Menelaos' efforts to bring her back mean one thing to Menelaos, quite another to Orestes, and the difference is crucial.

   The phrasing of Menelaos' lament (compare ll. 1574–76) gives Orestes (and Euripides) the opportunity of calling to mind the episode described in the note to lines 1319–21: if Menelaos were man enough, he would have gotten Helen back not to enjoy her again but to punish her for her adultery. "If only it were so!" means, then, "If only you had gone to all that trouble *in order to kill her,* but everyone knows why you took the trouble, being the sort of man you are." The subtlety of this retort may have opened the way first to misunderstanding, then to changes in the text, especially at lines 1654–59.

1692–99 The most suspenseful moment in the play: Menelaos seems to surrender, and Orestes to accept it with another insult (l. 1692). As Menelaos makes no further effort after line 1692, Orestes presses on, giving the command to fire the palace but not, yet, moving to carry out his threat against Hermione. Menelaos, instead of capitulating before the palace is torched, and possibly because he senses Orestes' reluctance to kill Hermione, orders his men to advance against it. Everything is about to collapse, leaving Helen apparently and Orestes certainly dead in Argos (contrary to both their traditional fates) when Apollo appears above the palace. A spectacular finale, to say the least.

1694 *most loyal of all my friends* The compliment to the loyalty of Pylades is doubly appropriate: (a) Menelaos' treachery stands out in stark contrast against it; (b) Orestes' last words to his friend in the play remind us of what he said when he first saw him enter. The contrast with Menelaos is implicit in the earlier passage too (ll. 758–65).

1696 *Land of Danaos, of the founders and their horses!* Not necessarily a sign that Argive troops are approaching: Helen had called on Argos from within the palace (l. 1328), so, too, Electra at the start of her lament (l. 994).

1697 *Come on, Argives, bring your weapons, hurry!* The men who respond to this exhortation are most likely the men ordered to attack the doors at line 1637. See previous note.

1709 *For the daughter of imperishable Zeus must not perish* Helen's status as daughter of Zeus first appears at line 1422. It emerges at key points twice in the Phrygian episode (ll. 1486, 1563), where the form employed for Zeus' name is *Dios*. Here Euripides employs the dialectal form *Zenos* in order to make a pun between the root of the name (*Zen-*) and the infinitive (*zen*, ["to live"]). Helen owes her salvation from death directly to her connection with Zeus, indirectly to the coincidental resemblance between the root of Zeus' name and the word for life.

    The similarity between *zen* ("to live") and *Zen-* in *Zenos* ("of Zeus") is purely fortuitous from an etymological point of view, but such chance resemblances between words were taken seriously by the ancients. For another example in this play, see note on line 993.

1714 *Parrhasia* In southern Arcadia.

1719 *the Areopagos* "The Hill of Ares" in Athens, site of the court for the trial of homicides.

1721–27 Electra's marriage to Pylades has been well prepared (ll. 1129–31, 1141–43, 1252–55); the match between Orestes and Hermione would not have troubled the original audience (it would have been familiar from Euripides' *Andromache,* if not from other sources as well). Of greater importance, Euripides has portrayed Orestes at the apparent nadir of his fortunes as a youth tragically deprived of the opportunity to experience the joys of marriage and children (ll. 1079–1100). Marriage is the logical culmination of a play that ends positively for an adolescent hero, especially one who has suffered so much in his encounter with the female sex (see my introduction, section VI).

1723–26 Neoptolemos, the son of Achilles, is depicted as betrothed to Hermione in Homer's *Odyssey* (4.5–9). After the Trojan War, however, Neoptolemos went to Delphi to take Apollo to task for bringing about the death of Achilles, and there he perished, evidently before he could marry Hermione.

1728 *Menelaos, let Orestes reign here in Argos* Confirms the suspicion, expressed by Orestes at 1107–8, that Menelaos has had designs on the throne of Argos.

1733–36 According to the *Kypria,* one of the "cyclic" epic poems rounding out the story of the Trojan War, Zeus decides to relieve the earth of its excessive population. The war occasioned by Helen's elopement with Paris is the means employed.

1733 *the gods, by means of this one's beauty*   As Helen herself implies at line 91, she has been an instrument of divine intention all along (see note on l. 1425).

1737–39 Orestes' strongest point in his self-defense (ll. 612–21) is the only one Apollo advances. Menelaos had criticized it (ll. 418–19) and the Argive assembly, to judge from the messenger's last utterance (see note on ll. 992–93), had not been persuaded by it. Now both are compelled to admit its truth and to accept its exculpatory value.

1742–43 *thinking what I heard / as your voice was really some fiend's*   A new disclosure, not to be taken ironically (see my introduction, section XI).

1755 *Loxias*   Another name for Apollo.

1757 *honoring Peace, loveliest of the gods*   That is, getting along with one another: the strife that has been the play has come to an end. Perhaps also the poet's implicit advice to his fellow citizens: they had rejected peace on favorable terms with Sparta two years before, after the victory at Kyzikos.

1760–61 *Hebe, / the wife of Herakles*   Hebe is the daughter of Zeus and Hera. Her name means Youth. Herakles is the son of Zeus and the mortal Alkmene, famed for his Twelve Labors and rewarded for them with exaltation to divine status after his death. Euripides is careful to escort the deified Helen into an Olympus peopled with former mortals: Herakles here and her own brothers at lines 1710 and 1765.

1768–70 The chorus has the last word, a prayer that the play now over will find favor with the judges. We do not know how *Orestes* fared with the judges at its original performance. On its popularity afterwards, see my introduction, section V.

GLOSSARY

AEROPE: daughter of Katreus, king of Crete. Married to Atreus, she becomes the mother of Agamemnon and Menelaos but commits adultery with her husband's brother Thyestes.

AGAMEMNON: son of Atreus and father of Orestes and Electra. King of Argos and leader of the Greeks against Troy, he is murdered, on his return, by his wife, Clytemnestra.

AIGISTHOS: son of Thyestes. He becomes the lover of Agamemnon's wife, Clytemnestra, while Agamemnon is away at Troy and helps her kill him and seize the throne on his return. He is then killed by Orestes.

APOLLO: son of Zeus and Leto, Greek god of prophecy delivered from his oracle at Delphi. It is at Delphi that Orestes receives the command to kill his mother Clytemnestra.

ARGOS: a city in the Argive plain, three miles from the sea. Home of Agamemnon, scene of our play. Often confused by the Greek tragedians with Mycenae, which it conquered in 468 B.C.

ATREUS: son of Pelops, husband of Aerope who bears him Agamemnon and Menelaos. Best known for the revenge he takes on his brother Thyestes, who seduces his wife Aerope: pretending reconciliation, he feeds the unsuspecting Thyestes the flesh of his own children.

AULIS: point of embarkation for the Greek fleet on its way to Troy.

CASTOR: Mortal son of Tyndareos and Leda, full brother of Clytemnestra, half brother of Helen and Polydeukes.

CLYTEMNESTRA: daughter of Tyndareos and Leda, half sister of Helen and Polydeukes, full sister of Castor. Having murdered her husband Agamemnon on his return from Troy, she is killed in turn by her son Orestes.

DELPHI: seat of the famous oracle of Apollo on Mount Parnassus, about two thousand feet above the Gulf of Corinth. Also called Pytho (hence Apollo's epithet, Pythian).

ELECTRA: daughter of Agamemnon and Clytemnestra. She helps her brother Orestes kill Clytemnestra.

EUMENIDES: the kindly ones, a euphemism for the *Erinyes* (Furies), dread powers of the underworld. Daughters of Earth according to Hesiod, of Night according to Aeschylus; avengers of crimes committed against kindred, they pursue and madden Orestes after he murders his mother.

FURIES: see Eumenides

HADES: god of death and of the dead; his name is used also for the underworld, the place of the dead.

HELEN: daughter of Zeus and Leda, queen of Sparta, half sister of Clytemnestra and Castor, full sister of Polydeukes. Though her real father is Zeus, she is often referred to as the daughter of Tyndareos, her mother's husband. Abandoning her own husband, Menelaos, she elopes with the Trojan prince Paris, thus causing the Trojan War.

HERMIONE: daughter of Menelaos and Helen.

IPHIGENEIA: daughter of Agamemnon and Clytemnestra, sacrificed by her father at Aulis to secure favorable winds for the journey of the Greek fleet to Troy.

LEDA: wife of Tyndareos, mother by him of Clytemnestra and Castor; to Zeus, who comes to her in the form of a swan, she bears Helen and Polydeukes.

MENELAOS: son of Atreus and brother of Agamemnon. As husband of Helen, Menelaos is lord of Sparta.

MYCENAE: a city about six miles north of Argos, with which it is often confused in Greek tragedy.

MYRTILOS: son of Hermes, cast by Pelops into the sea.

NAUPLIA: the port of Argos, about seven miles from the city.

ORESTES: son of Agamemnon and Clytemnestra, he kills his mother to avenge her murder of his father.

PELASGIA: traditional name for Argos. The adjective Pelasgian means little more than very ancient, the Pelasgians being the pre-Hellenic inhabitants of Greece.

PELOPS: son of Tantalos and Dione, father of Atreus and Thyestes. The Peloponnesus ("island of Pelops") is named after him.

PHOKIS: a region of central Greece, in the vicinity of Mount Parnassus, home of Orestes' friend Pylades.

POLYDEUKES: Immortal son of Zeus and Leda, full brother of Helen, half brother of Castor and Clytemnestra.

PYLADES: son of Strophios, cousin and close friend of Orestes.

PYTHIAN: epithet of Apollo as god of the oracle at Delphi, which see.

SPARTA: a city in the central Peloponnesus, on the west bank of the Eurotas river, home of Helen and Menelaos.

STROPHIOS: father of Pylades.

TANTALIDS: descendants of Tantalos.

TANTALOS: son of Zeus and Pluto (the rich), king of Lydia, a land famed for its gold. Ancient prototype of excessive good fortune issuing in disaster. Progenitor of the dynasty whose last living members are Orestes and Electra.

THYESTES: son of Pelops, brother of Atreus whose wife, Aerope, he seduces. Tricked by Atreus into eating the flesh of his own sons, he begets another son, Aigisthos, to be his avenger in the next generation.

TROY: the famous city in Asia Minor, site of the Trojan War fought by the Greeks to retrieve Helen.

TYNDAREOS: king of Sparta, husband of Leda and father of Clytemnestra and Castor; Leda's other two children, Helen and Polydeukes, had Zeus for their father. The brothers, however, are often called both Sons of Tyndareos and Sons of Zeus. Helen, too, appears as his daughter.

TYNDARIDAI: Castor and Polydeukes, the Sons of Tyndareos.

ZEUS: chief god of Greek religion and mythology, father of Apollo, Tantalos, and Helen.